THE NEW FORESTS

WILDLIFE WITHIN OUR COMMERCIAL WOODLANDS

BY DAVE LOCK

For Chris.

A PINEBRANCH PRODUCTION

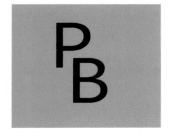

www.davelockpics.com

CONTENTS

CLEARFELL   PG 9

TREE PIPIT   11

NIGHTJAR   18

ROE DEER   27

NEW PLANTINGS   31

REDPOLL   34

WHINCHAT   40
JUST COMMON BIRDS?   15

WHY WERE THE FORESTS CREATED?   24

RIGHT OR WRONG?   36

POLE STAGE   69

GOLDCREST   70

LONG EARED OWL   77

THE SPARROWHAWK   80

COAL TIT   86

STUDIES WITHIN THE FORESTS   72

THE EDGE EFFECT   84

ROADS AND PATHSWAYS   88

BIBLIOGRAPHY/FURTHER READING   146

THICKET   PG 45

WHITETHROAT AND LINNET   46

BLACK GROUSE   49

FALLOW DEER   53

UNOFICIAL NATURE RESERVES   52

WATER   58

MATURE WOODLAND   92

GOSHAWK   94

CROSSBILL   104

RED DEER   113

SISKIN   119

RED SQUIRREL   125

CALEDONIA;   131

CAPERCAILLIE   133

PINE MARTEN   139

WINTER IN THE FORESTS   102

HIGH SUMMER   137

THE FUTURE OF FORESTRY   115

RESTRUCTURING   121

Introduction

Over the last century, woodlands have been created in Britain to fill in our insatiable demand for timber. These New Forests are mainly comprised of introduced coniferous trees from other parts of the world and are found all around our shores. Not to everyone's tastes, they have been controversial to many people from Politicians, Conservationists, and to lovers of all natural. For our Wildlife, they are safe havens, for both our common species and specialists that can be found within. This book highlights the coniferous enclave, and illustrates some of its inhabitants.

Attempting to supply the UK with its own supply of timber, it is realized that we cannot expect other parts of the world to export their natural resources just for our gain. To many it seems unethical that we use that resource, unless it becomes repeatedly beneficial for them. Indeed the 'developed' world should look inward and work to tilt the balance, and become more sustainable. The British Forestry industry has actively pursued this ideal, and although it may have a long way to go, it may never become totally self sufficient however, but reach a certain level or amount.

The established industry has developed many tried and tested methods of managing its woodlands for optimum growth and harvest, with the most used method being the Clear cut or clearfell system, which is highlighted here. This method not only provides a sustainable yield, where the forest provides timber, but it also allows permanent opportunity for a range of wildlife to flourish. In areas where this method is not used on such a big scale, the presence of conifer trees on their own is enough to attract a diverse and sometimes rare group of animals.

The Cycle:

This process of course starts with the initial planting of the crop. This afforestation could be on recently acquired land, or as is more commonly found in these times, on land that has recently been harvested (re-stocking). An open aspect is created at this time. Once the trees have become established, after a few years they grow into the thicket stage, where the trees are touching themselves and begin to dominate any surrounding grass and herbaceous vegetation: Reaching two or three meters in height.

Come back to the same patch some years later, and we see that the trees have grown above our heads and have reached the Pole stage. The lower branches on some species of conifer tree die off as they gain height, so we are presented with rows of even-aged trunks and a closed canopy. Other trees offer a wall of green foliage: Often a dark and forbidding place to try and enter.

Years later, they will reach maturity, and it is noticed that since then, some trees have been removed as part of the harvest, which gives the final stand more room to grow up and outward.

So where can we find these New Forests? Take a drive, or travel around any county or region within the British Isles, and at some point a familiar green belt of 'Christmas trees' will come into view. You probably already know of their existence. Places of solitude and recreation, the green name–plated woodlands we have all have spent some time within.

This industrial aspect of supplying timber on such a large scale is seen by some as unnatural in its visual impact on our countryside however, and moves are already afoot in changing a system that can and does already support wildlife. Forestry has always been a controversial subject in the way it works, with politicians, environmentalists and the general public all having a say. Will the future of forestry, with its initial thoughts of supplying Britain with some of its timber needs along with conservation aims, change *its* nature in the coming years?

Clearfell

Machines have cut and stacked the wood that was previously a mature conifer forest and Lorries have started to carry the timbers away for further processing. Now it is time for the next rotation. But before this happens, more mechanization is needed to prepare the ground for replanting. Powerful scarifying machines and diggers cut channels within the stumps of the former inhabiting trees, pushing aside everything that was discarded by the cutters. What is left could be described as a re-enactment of World War 1- thankfully without any soldiers.

Trying to get across this clear-felled landscape is in itself difficult, unless you can follow the lines where the machines have been, because the brash (left-over branches from the trunks themselves), and stumps, usually form foot-wrenching barriers to the walker. This derelict site of apparent sterility would appear to be a deterrent to wildlife, but on closer study, we find it is offers an ideal foothold for 'forest' animals.

Before we dismiss this cleansed and apparently barren area as just waste-land, (which is what some people perceive these new coniferous forests to be) let us ask ourselves, what value do they have as regarding wildlife interest? The reply to this could be: What do these areas resemble elsewhere? What habitat has been created by the action of the forester?

Looking from this angle, we can give ourselves a hint as to what we may find.

Structurally, the clearfell site resembles open ground, perhaps Heathland, or in some instances as in the uplands, rough moorland: exactly what some of these areas were before they were planted. In establishing this type of similar environment, they then attract similar creatures. Interestingly some of them rare and formerly displaced from their usual habitats elsewhere. From this viewpoint, then they attain value.

Indeed in some parts of Britain, Forest Enterprise, or the Forestry Commission (FC), has embarked on a program of regeneration, in some cases turning back clearfell sites back to former heathland, for example, rather than replanting again with commercial timber interests. This may be a sign of the present conservation influences and economics of today.

In any case, the establishment of the clearfell site has provided an opportunity for birds and other animals that prefer open ground. Contravening the situation that is all too uncommon in times where land such as this is viewed with a mind for development.

How long this regime will continue we cannot be truthful in predicting, because the forestry animal is an old, constantly changing beast that responds to the attitude of the time. It is likely however that this conserving attitude will prevail, with any further increase in timber output coming not from fresh new conifer forests that are newly planted, but rather than using the forests that are already established. Because of this re-use or rotational aspect that is employed in the clearfell method, different age and height structures are created. Initially, we may not have been aware of how beneficial this could be, as this aspect encourages diversity.

WHEN TREES ARE FELLED

First rotation tree felling can be seen generally as the start of the building of a varied habitat. Just how this is achieved obviously needs planning, although economic chances at the times may play a part. To form this varied habitat structure, it is not necessary for the whole of the forest to cut at once. These variations are often brought about by harvesting being earlier than planned, or delayed even with the fact that the tree has come to the end of its optimum growth, and so just a section is felled creating this variety in structure. Being part of a sustainable process, the amount that is available to cut is equal to the amount that is regenerated in that year with growth, so the total amount of timber that remains is the same if fully stocked. Sometimes the cut is less if the woodland needs to be built up if thought to be under-stocked, or the amount cut increased if overstocked, so some of the capitol (the total amount of the wood in the forest) can be cashed in. As a matter of course, over the years, as mentioned, this process has been seen to be beneficial through these various management techniques as being a plus-point for wildlife. This welfare for wildlife becoming more prevalent, as we as a nation become more concerned about the environment.

Tree Pipit

If you take a walk around a patch of clearfell in springtime, perhaps you will come across a Tree Pipit. The birds arrive from their African winter quarters arriving in the warmer months of our temperate climate, and are here to breed, arriving around the beginning of April. They can be found on most open ground around the British Isles and although rarer in Ireland, have taken a shine to clearfell as areas in which to settle.

The male is noticeable through his method of display. He takes off from a nearby tree or log, calling in a slow staccato song, rising upward, to a height of perhaps a hundred feet. Parachuting down on fluttering wings, he delivers a descending trill, which catches your attention.

Could you consider the Tree Pipit a bird of the woodlands? Perhaps not in the true sense of say a Woodpecker is - dependent of trees as a whole, but it has found that it can live within the boundaries of the conifer woodlands themselves.

The Tree Pipit has a musical song, usually delivered form high, on the wing.
The nest itself is hidden, tucked away on the floor of the clearfell.

Closer observation will show that with time, other Pipits will come into the patch. They can be other males, in which they will be chased away, or courted if female.

When the birds do settle down, then nest building begins, which is constructed on the ground, hidden under a tussock of grass, a plant, or perhaps a divot that has been turned by the diggers. The grass bowl structure,is lined with finer moss and hair.

Interestingly, the five or so eggs that are laid show remarkable variation in their colour from one clutch to another.

About ¾ of an inch long, the ground colours vary from buff, blue, or pink, and can be streaked with brown, black or claret markings. Some are darker, with a smudged appearance. It is not surprising with such variation that it is a favoured target for the Cuckoo in its parasitism.

Some interesting behaviour has been noted, in that the male will chase its mate back to the nest if it thinks she has spent too much time off, and should carry on with the incubation.

When the eggs have hatched after about 14 days, then activity increases as the adults find food for their offspring. The adults will mostly fly off to other areas on the clearfell - where they have previously found food and collect beak-fulls of insects to satisfy the offspring's hungry mouths.

Very often, they collect food as they walk about the ground, picking flies and beetles from the low foliage, sometimes only a few feet from the nest itself. They walk into the nest site, rather than fly, which helps to conceal its location from predators.

The young leave the nest after about two weeks, and still continue to be fed by the parents for a while, the adult pair often keen on starting another clutch, before flying back to Africa before the onset of colder weather.

Predation can come in many forms on the clearfell; avian, reptilian and mammalian opportunists are all looking for the possibility of a meal on the site. The birds have to be vigilant to avoid these opportunists. Night time enemies are on the lookout too. Stoat, Adder and Tawny Owl can snatch adult and young if they become noticeable.

The actual status of the bird can be confusing. In Wales it is fairly common albeit local in distribution because of its liking for commercial forestry. In Scotland, it has recently been added as a Scottish Natural Heritage Biodiversity Indicator. Because of their visibility, some birds are used to indicate climate change, if they are reasonably widespread and well recorded. On the flip side to this though, Tree Pipits are designated red in the current listing of the IUCN although with least concern.

The adults usually walk in to the nest with food. This in the hope of avoiding predators.

JUST COMMON BIRDS ?

The Tree Pipit is one bird that has taken to the new clearfell sites for breeding and feeding areas, but what of other species? The variety that can be found as vegetation starts to get a grip increases. Studies show this, and it is fair to say that most birds will use commercial forestry at varying stages in which to live and nest at some point.

We could argue that these species are just common birds that could be seen anywhere, which is probably true, but in these times where habitat is being lost through increasing urbanization and changing farming methods, then forest areas play a big part in holding significant populations of what are regarded as common or farmland birds.

It becomes apparent that the forests have become sanctuaries for birds as other habitats have degraded. Nature adapts, and the relatively new habitats that have been created have attracted species, as they have mirrored their usually dependant homelands. Clearfell compared to Heathlands, for example. Also, these New Forests have created opportunities that did not exist before, and thus have attracted new colonisers such as the Common Crossbill.

Some studies have been carried out and the results have been surprising in the least. In the 1980's for example, over thirty species were counted on Welsh second rotation, or re-stocks within the forests, with Willow warbler being the most numerous. This puts the general argument for the fact that commercial forests are of no interests in doubt, and important populations live within this environment.

Most birds will use commercial forest in which to live. The Greater Spotted Woodpecker and the Song Thrush are two.

Obviously, it is just a matter of course that clearfell will be created because the valuable timber has to be harvested, and is this not the aim of the exercise? Following, replanting is carried on after the harvest to maintain stock; the business of forestry.

It is the successive stages that this commercial silviculture creates that provide valuable habitats not just for common birds and animals, but for those specialists that would not be there if forestry had not been started. Indeed, it could also be a lifesaver to some birds and animals that these habitats exist. It could be argued that a number of species that live in the commercial forestry environment would only be hanging on as part of our fauna, if the forests were not there.

The Chaffinch is probably the commonist finch found within the forests, especially in upland situations.

It is not too long before we can see vegetation starting to come through on the clearfell along with the newly planted saplings. If larch was there before, then grasses and other plants such as Bramble are probably there already. If denser Spruce was the previous mainstay, then wind-blown plants and dormant seeds that have been present perhaps for decades, will soon start to show when light is available. As the ground flora starts to get a hold amongst the conifer saplings that have recently been planted, then animal colonists from the surrounding plots of varying age take advantage as long as they find it to their liking. Foxes that lie up in mature stands in the day, may find that the Voles and Shrews that have moved into a restocked area, provide food for example. Migrant birds such as Willow Warbler and Chiffchaff like to use the tangle of shrub and forest edge to nest. Then there are birds that require a particular habitat, created by harvesting, such as the Nightjar.

NIGHTJAR

You will have to look for the Nightjar towards the end of the day, in the springtime or summer months, in order to experience this African visitor. Checking out a patch of clearfell, the Nightjar will more than likely be heard before it is seen, but it is a good starting point in tracking what areas will most likely be occupied. The famous churring contact call may be reward enough to some birdwatchers, but with patience the birds can be viewed in the dying glow of the evening. A bird of the night - starting at twilight, this crepuscular bird can be seen, flying moth-like, on the open clear fell sites and roads around the conifer forests.

It has traditionally been a bird of heathland areas, noticeably in the southern part of the British Isles - its stronghold in former times, but clearfell sites across Britain are popular as breeding ground for this cryptically coloured insect-hoover.

An insect- hoover could be an apt description, especially in describing the way it feeds. The bird flies around the clearfell, open-mouthed along the forest edge, scooping up its insectivorous food. To this end, the bird is marvelously adapted for this. Its gape is very large, and the size seams to be expanded in design with a fringe of bristles that help to funnel-in its prey.

As a bird of the night, it has to make the best of whatever light is available and to this end, in appearance, it doesn't disappoint with large pools of dark oversized eyes: Owl-like in appearance. Overall, the bird is cryptically covered with a brown mottle and patches of grey, buff-white and black. Both the male and female are alike, with the former having large pale spots on each wing and outer tail. All this camouflage help to blend the birds into its background as they lie on the ground, or on an a lateral branch. Indeed it is almost impossible to see as it resembles a piece of bark or brash that has been left after the trees have been previously cut and stripped. Here it remains stock-still, perhaps roosting whilst incubating. Its eyes shut tight.

Arriving in May, it isn't long before pairs establish themselves, and start to breed. As well as the audible churring, designed to advertise its presence to others of its kind, the male has a display flight which involves an unusual "coi coi" or "hoop" sounding call coupled with wing clapping.

The bird dispenses with the formalities of nest building, saving time and energy by laying their clutch of two eggs directly on the ground. Unusually shaped, they are long and pebble-like in appearance. Ground coloured in cream or white, covered in lines of lead grey, black and brown. There can be two clutches by the time they fly back to warmer parts in late August or September, before winter is upon us.

The two downy young, which hatch after eighteen days or so, are shielded by its parent bird during the day from the elements whether they be sun, wind or rain; unusually with the remains of the eggshells still nearby. The birds sitting close and still dependent on the disruptive colouration of its camouflage as its defense.

During daylight hours Nightjar and their young remain still and rely on their camoflague to blend in. Eggshells are not carried away as generally they are with other birds, but are left out at the nest area. The rim of bristles around the adults' gape which help catch insects are visible.

Although motionless during the day, it is towards night time that the bird becomes active, just as the sun dies. Understandably, after a day of immobility, the small young birds are hungry and impatient.The adult bird also becomes more alert at this time, with its dark eyes becoming apparent; usually flying off when its mate arrives after the first hunting forey, the newcomer starting to feed the two ravenous youngsters.
It does this by regurgitating insect matter it has caught, which is partially digested in appearance, and as each chick stands either side of its parents beak, they feed taking in the food simultaneously. Pigeons also feed similarly in this way, but of course, they eat partially digested vegetable matter.

There are many predators on the clearfell. The Stoat is one of them.

Nightjars have had an up and down status over the years regarding their general population within the British Isles. Recent studies however have shown that they are coming back in number since the middle of the last century, when their southern heathland strongholds were swallowed up: viewed as prime sites for development and conversion into farmland.

By coincidence, it is the process of clear felling that has lent to their requirements, providing suitable habitat over most parts of Britain. In more recent times, some of those areas that were planted up with conifer, are being returned to heathland, which will not only provide more permanent sites for the birds, but for other animals such as reptiles and insects that specialize in this type of habitat. However, as long as there are areas of clearfell generated as part of the forestry process, then there should be room for Nightjar.

From 1992 until 2004, Nightjar have increased some 34%, with the big numbers still in the south, and it is interesting that an action plan has outlined that clearfell must still form a significant part of its status, if we wish to see a healthy population of this enigmatic bird within our shores.

Two chicks are fed simultaniously by the adult, each lining up side-by-side in front of the parent.

The male flies in to feed the young after the female leaves to hunt.

Why Were The Forests Created?

The forests that we find around many parts of Britain today, are very different to what they were in times past. The woodlands that have been created relatively recently, containing mostly conifers, are not the wild woods of our imagination or those worked in to supply wood for charcoal or crafted household furniture - the deciduous broadleaf that inhabited Britain some hundred years ago: before these regimented blocks of even-aged trees had been planted, or have been harvested and since replaced with more of the same. But how did they become part of our countryside? And why has this type of woodland become so important?

It all started in the 1900's, when just after the First World War it became apparent that Britain needed to become more sufficient in providing its own timber. At this time, only some 5% of our land was actually covered with woodlands, and we were reliant mainly on imports in meeting our needs. The British Empire was breaking up, and we could not rely as we did in years past on milking countries far and wide for their timber. This was highlighted with the war effort, when timber importing was difficult, due to merchant shipping being sunk by the German Navy.

The answer to this was the creation of the Forestry Commission (FC), a government body which would oversee the creation of new forests, and promote others who would like to do the same. Of course, it had to fit in with other demands that we thought of as important at this time: agriculture, the development of towns and cities, expanding road infrastructures, for example. It also meant that the initial forests had to use marginal, non-productive lands that perhaps were difficult to cultivate, were not generally thought of as much use - and were cheap.

The Commission had of course the main objective of establishing timber supplies, and it still does this through a number of ways. It promotes the establishment of woodland by outside interests such as farmers, landowners and independent forestry businesses through grants which it oversees.

It likewise issues licenses when woodland needs trimming or felling, providing a plan of operations. Significantly, it also set up a large, state-owned forest system.

With this in mind, it became apparent that the timber that was needed had to grow fast, and be of a certain useable shape and size to meet the needs of an expanding population.

To this end, the New Forests that were created were to be found in upland hilly country such as in Scotland, Wales and Northern England, the sandy Brecks of East Anglia or the Heath lands of the South. Soon, great swathes of countryside were under trees that were imported from countries such as Scandinavia, North America and the Orient. These trees were perceived to be ideal for our warm wet climate, and it was hoped that it would not be too long before we could reap the benefits.

The timber created in these New Forests has had differing end uses over the Forestry Commissions' conception. In the first years, one priority was to grow props for the huge coal industry: The powerhouse of Britain in the early part of the twentieth century. The uses have changed over time, and now the straight timbers of our forests are used for example in the construction industry, and as components for the many forms of fiber board used in building and furniture. Of course there will always be a market for pulp used in print and packaging operations. Britain also exports some of its forestry products. Over 460 green tones of round wood and over 130 thousand tones of chip were exported in 2011. No matter what ingenious uses we find in reconstituting wood in another form, or just plainly using timber for what it is, there will always be a demand for it.

Deer

Deer are found extensively around the New Forests of Britain. Most people are unaware of their presence as they live shy and retiring lives. Three main species can be found in good number: The Fallow, Red and the Roe. Most have been introduced to these shores at various times in the past, with some quite recently. These in the main have formed collections to adorn large estates and satisfy those who enjoy the animals just for what they are. Then they escape or are deliberately set free, and over time, establish themselves in small pockets around the country. There is no doubt that the state-owned commercial forests have, and still are playing a large part in their expansion around the country, along with their welfare. Deer are mentioned in various chapters within this book, as they are not just specific to one stage of forestry, but rather make use of the whole forest in which to live.

In a lot of cases within the commercial forest enclave, deer are seen as a pest, and as a result are constantly being controlled. Being browsing animals, they live off the trees themselves, as well as any other herbage that is growing within our network of unofficial nature reserves.

Roe Deer Twins

Roe Deer

The Roe Deer is a native to our Islands, unlike most of the other small deer found in the countryside.

More of a solitary animal, the Roe can generally be seen more easily than the Fallow, as it leaves the sanctuary of the forest to browse on suitable adjoining open ground. They sometimes can be stumbled upon walking through the network of paths within the forest, whereupon at a safe distance after taking flight, they will stop to look back, and perhaps bark a distinct warning. Found across the British Isles, although largely absent from Wales, it is commonly found instead of the Fallow in most of Scotland. Usually being on their own, they have not the eyes and ears of their fellows to help keep watch as do Red Deer, for example. Perhaps it is this situation that may make them more noticeable. The car is also a good way of seeing the deer, as driving along suitable places sometimes allow an approach, acting as a portable hide.

Females usually give birth to twins, one of which can be just seen, hidden to the mothers left.

In wintertime, they are more secretive, and spend more of their time within the forest, but in spring and summer, they can be seen during morning and evening searching for food amongst the agricultural lands that surround the commercial woodlands. Once out in the open it can be more sociable, and can be seen in groups.

A small deer, reaching between 60 and75 cm in height, it could be described as the 'Bambi' of the deer species. Generally a rich brown in colour, the adults lack the spots of the common variety of the Fallow. The coat is a greyer tone in the winter months. The bigger size of the Red will rule out any confusion.

The buck lacks the antlers of the Red or the Fallow, but does possess a small set of prongs, with three points or tines.

The rut, where the male seeks to attract female attention with the aim of breeding, begins in mid July and lasts till the end of August. He can get aggressive at this time, defending a territory, scent marking against branches and herbage in competition with other males. Fights do occur, with males locking antlers, pushing and shoving.

The Buck in attracting female company has his own version of an arena similar to the Fallow Deer. Unlike the rutting stand or area of the Fallow, the Roe has a ring shaped course in which he runs around. There is usually a tree or bush in its center, and perhaps two of these rings may form an '8' in shape, all in the hope of impressing the females.

When mated, the female experiences delayed implantation which is usually found in smaller mammals. The Roe deer is the only hoofed animal which uses this process. It has a nine months gestation period, four of which the embryo does not develop, so it only grows for five, starting in January.

Usually twins are born, dappled in colour, which when not being suckled are frequently left alone, apart, hidden in grass or some other long herbage. They can stay with their mothers well into the following winter, and become sexually mature at 14 months.

Another deer that is controlled by fencing and shooting, many fall victim to road traffic. Viewed as a pest within forestry, there could be as many as 500,000 within the British Isles.

NEW PLANTINGS:
A TALE OF WHAT WAS AND WHAT WE COULD EXPECT.

In theory, this should chronologically be the start of the process of coniferous forestry. However, as in nature itself, like all living things, the forestry management process is evolving. Its policies are changing seemingly each decade as new ideas and methods, as well as public and political input, all push the way forestry should be going. To this end, up to recent times, very little new virgin ground has been acquired by the Forestry Commission and planted with conifer trees in both England and Wales. Only Scotland has utilized new ground in recent years. Even then, the annual total of new planting has decreased. Most new conifer tree planting seen today, is via restocking.

Obviously, it has not all been like this, as the initial idea was for Britain to be as self-sufficient as well as it could be in its conception in the early 1900"s, so all new forests were on newly acquired land.

It has to be said, that compulsory purchase has never been the policy of acquiring such lands, and voluntary sales have led the way. Also, there are large sectors of forestry in which leasing the land also play their part in making up the total area of new forestry. Grant aid plays a big part as incentive to persuade land owners to turn to forestry.

Initially, planting the forests were concentrated on marginal lands, such as the drier and less productive places such as Heath, or countryside that was thought of as low agricultural interest. The wetter Uplands of Scotland, Wales and Northern England were seen as suitable, and it is here that the majority of planting has occurred.

Britain falls into the Taiga, transitional mixed forest and temperate broadleaf zones. With the bulk of the population and development being towards the south of the country, it seemed only natural to look at these marginal areas and realize that conifers fitted better in the north and west, with an increasing broadleaf element toward the east and south.

Not only just restricted to the Forestry Commission, private companies and landowners saw it as an opportunity to raise cash via timber harvesting in the future, aided with beneficial tax incentives. Indeed this idea of planting for profit was not a new one, as plantations were initiated in Perthshire for example, as far back as 1764 by the Duke of Atholl. Here Japanese and European Larch were planted, and after some time it was realized that a hardy hybrid between the two was born.

So what birds use these newly established forests? With their establishment mainly in the uplands, it became apparent that the birds that occupied them after planting were those that were already there; the moorland-loving variety.

Likewise, in other parts of Britain, such as in the East Anglian Brecklands, the species that could be found there previously, used the new plantations in the early years.

The true conifer specialists came later as the forests matured, but in those intervening years, birds were adaptable and the general species that we assume as farmland or moorland lovers for example, found the new areas to their liking. Perhaps only staying for a few years until the structure of the woodland outgrew their requirements.

In this situation, species such as Hen Harrier and Short Eared Owl, can adapt for a while. The short grass that exists within the forest at this time, and up to the pre-thicket stage, along with adjacent open land can provide the small mammals on which they feed and the seclusion they need in which to breed. Here they can be free from levels of persecution that they may generally experience outside the forest such as in game keeping areas, for example: to this day, an aspect that is still all too prevalent in holding back any population growth for animals of hooked beak and claw.

In other non-upland areas, this pattern was replicated. Birds such as Nightjar and Woodlark could be found within the New Forests of Lowland Britain and although eventually the growing structure meant that these areas became unsuitable, they could provide some space for them in which to live. For a long time, forestry has had the finger of blame often pointed towards it as a reason for the general demise of wildlife due to land use change, but in lowland Britain, general urbanization and Agricultural improvements have also played their parts. In the case of the Brecklands, the deterioration of heathland through grazing by sheep, and the use of myxomatosis in rabbit control, has changed its nature. With the positive attitude that we now see regarding wildlife and its welfare, areas of forestry are being modified to attract these rare breeding birds and other animals in providing a safe haven. Now they are seen as providing an active roll for wildlife welfare.

The Short Eared Owl is one hunter that can take advantage of newly-planted forestry.

Lesser Redpoll

The Redpoll was a rare bird before the inclusion of the New Forests within the British Isles. A northern bird of the past, it is generally found predominantly around pioneering Birch forests and scrub. With the change of open moorland habitat and the creation of coniferous plantations around poorer farmland in the south, the Redpoll has had almost as meteoric a spread as the Siskin, in taking to the newly planted forest enclaves. Whereas other birds such as its 'cousin' took advantage of the forests as they became older, the Redpoll was able to move in when the trees were becoming established.

A finch with a small bill, it has developed its feeding to accommodate seeds such as Birch and Alder in the winter months, with herbaceous plants such as Sorrel, Chickweed and Dandelion in the Spring and summer. It also eats buds from flowering trees such as Larch. A bird which has a metallic "Ch-Chit" sound as it flies overhead, generally is a quiet inclusion to our avian bird life around the forest, as it can be local or thinly spread in its distribution, but like some other finches, it can be found in small groups. The male has a butterfly-like display similar to the Siskin as it attempts to attract a female in its breeding season.

It seems however, that the inclusion of Birch within the early stages of new forestry is important. This broadleaf is common in higher latitudes, so naturally the Redpoll took advantage and utilized this food plant in other parts of the country as it became available. The thicket-like habitat that new young plantations emulate has been to their liking as a nesting habitat, but unfortunately, with our conifer forests growing to maturity, the closing of the canopy has become detrimental to the bird. In some areas it has disappeared as a nester as regimes of weeding have removed trees such as Birch in young forestry, also leaving little for the bird to feed on in the winter months.

Evidence of this is borne from observations in southern British counties when the new forests were initially created, their numbers increased, only to fall away as the forests developed and weeding and clearing regimes were introduced. The continuous-cover policies that are being developed in some locations, where young plantations will be phased out, will be detrimental to the Redpoll, and the bird may only hang on in some areas where Birch and scrub are allowed to prevail.

Numbers of Redpoll can be bolstered in the southern part of Britain during the winter period as those birds in the north move to the south to find new feeding opportunities, this movement being part of a regular migratory pattern. As with other seed eating Finches, their lives are geared around food availability and naturally migrate to areas other than those they favour just for breeding. They may stay in Britain if the winter seed crop of Birch and Alder is good, or if they are attracted to suitable supplies of Larch, but in some years they may wander further afield than our islands and travel to southern Europe. Here, within our forests in these colder months, they can be found in mixed flocks along with Siskin, Goldfinch and Tits feeding amongst our woodlands of Birch and conifers.

R i g h t   O r   W r o n g ?

Since planting of the New Forests initially began around the turn of the century, vast woodlands have been in existence around Britain. Policy of how planting was managed came to the forefront of public attention in the early 1980"s when the Forestry Commission granted permission to private companies to develop forestry in the Flow country of North Eastern Scotland.

It was at this time that the general public and conservation bodies were in uproar as acres of pristine moorland were beginning to be ploughed and planted with 'Alien' tree species from other countries. In their view, changing the whole aspect of these wilderness areas as upland bog was seen as being a mecca for breeding rarities such as Divers, Waders and Ducks.

Perhaps they had good reason to be angry. Unique communities which contain some of the rarest and interesting species of bird were under threat. On top of this, the whole process of planting was subsidized with tax relief to seemingly any party willing to invest; some being well known people of the time. This of course angered others not really that interested in wildlife issues, but made good reading in the tabloid press!

On reflection, maybe the area should not have been planted at all, as this corner of Britain is so unique. Even though the forests could have fitted into other less interesting areas there, if considered in the first place.

What the heated arguments over the situation did do however, was to focus not only conservationists into providing coherent argument for future possible conflicts of interest, whether it involved forestry or not, but it also affected Foresters in the same way. To this end, over the decades since, more co operation now exists between the Forestry Commission and interested conservation groups in managing future plans regarding forestry.

In hindsight, it has been a lesson well learned. Galvanizing public opinion has made the conservation bodies more effective, and movements that most people and politicians listen to. It has also revealed that there is still a lot to be learned about places like the flow country that are under threat, and that more research needs to be done here and in other habitats to quantify its wildlife value so that if confrontations in the future arise, there is hard data to back constructive argument.

Upland areas can be rich in wading birds such as the Redshank, and may need special consideration when forestry interests are intended.

For example, not all moorland is particularly attractive to common or particularly rare birds. It has been found that Greenshank prefer moors of a wetter aspect with certain plant preferences to rear its families on, whereas a few miles away, the aspect of moorland changes and waders show little interest in. Sheepwalk for example, is another habitat of this nature, and could be considered to be populated with less rare birds such as Meadow Pipit, and it is looking from this angle, aiming our studies along these lines that we can better understand what key sites are of particular value and should be allowed better protection. Moorlands may look the same everywhere, but on closer examination, they can be very different.

It is fair to say, that our state owned Forestry Commission, although regionalized, is now probably the largest land manager in the British Isles and has been extensively successful at producing timber for us all. Albeit as fast as it could, and perhaps with minimal thought for wildlife in general in the initial years, it must be realized however that then the thoughts of the public on wildlife welfare, and those of conservation organizations, were in their infancy compared to the powerful bodies they have become today. Generally wildlife was regarded as not as important as other more pressing issues of the day, with employment, economic growth and of course timber supplies all influencing policies.

Over time, with forward thinking towards conservation, it has been realized that the FC has a big part to play in what is a large chunk of how our wildlife fares. To this end, the Wildlife and Countryside Act was amended in 1985, to state that the Commission should consider a balanced view of both timber management and production, along with wildlife interests.

This trend for welfare has thankfully continued to be developed. The larger private companies that are operating, have also followed suit, and run their businesses on similar lines. Indeed, in some forests, it is difficult to see where Forestry Commission management ends, and private interests begin.

Much has been written, argued over and is still contentiously debated over the planting of conifer trees in our countryside, whether it is in the uplands, lowlands or the more populated areas of Britain. Some said to plant so much, in places that didn't need it, was deemed unnecessary. There are arguments for and against this from any angle one looks at it. Because of these previous contentions, commercial forests have attained a negative outlook by some. A paradox, as planting trees is generally looked on, by most of us, as a good thing.

The aspect of using our uplands for forest interests will seemingly always be a bone of contention. However with all cases complexities arise. For example, the Golden Eagle is

Upland forestry is often remote and seldom visited.

looked on as a symbol of what is truly wild, and requires large open tracts of 'empty' land, but if we are to accommodate their needs within forestry, at what stage do we look and judge an area to contain too much forestry (now or in the future) that would impede on its needs? They will accommodate some levels of forestry, but of course, a balanced view is needed.

Larch Cones

Whinchat

The Whinchat is a bird that can take advantage of the newly established forest because the habitat initially retains much of its previous characteristics. It also illustrates how some birds can adapt. This small spring and summer visitor is a migrant to our shores, and although it can be found on heath, the main area it settles is in our uplands. Nesting near or on the ground within herbage, it soon gets down to the business of breeding after its arrival in May, where it can if the weather is kind and when predation is not a factor, raise two broods before returning to its West African wintering grounds.

Insect of course form the main bulk of food for the nestlings, but in later months during the second brood, berries are in fruit and are often fed to the young.

The main reasons for birds that migrate to our islands, is of course to find food, and breed. Whinchats like a lot of small migrant birds are predominantly insect eaters and our uplands are a rich source of supply. For growing nestlings, these various high protein insects form the bulk of their food, but occasionally, berries and seeds are eaten.

The habitat which attracts the bird comprises of a mix of Heather, Bilberry and grass, with the latter being a favourite, all of which can persist in the space between and surrounding new plantings.

The physical presence of the forest and its inhabitants must influence the members of the adjacent open ground, and the Whinchat is no exception. Recent studies have shown although they are predated by members of the Crow family, Stoats and even Adders, which have a direct impact on eggs and nestlings and may be present even though no forestry in nearby, some predatory birds of the nearby forest can take adult Whinchats. Leg rings recovered from old nests of Sparrowhawks in South Wales show that they can form part of their diet.

Both the Whinchat, and its resident cousin the Stonechat take advantage of the early stages of afforestation. In forest predominantly with an underlying grass habitat, up to 20 pairs per sq/km can be found. In other upland plantations, up to 100 pairs per sq/km have been noted.

Adders are common predators for the Whinchat to look out for.

The general trend however, is that the bird on the whole has declined slightly in population terms over the last few decades. Having an amber status which although not of major concern, at least highlights this downward trend. Lowland populations have suffered through loss of marginal lands such as heath, in which it is also found, along with losses at egg and nestling stages perhaps through bad weather and predation here.

Presently

Today, the flavour of any new planting in the lowlands seems to be geared with Broadleaf trees. The interest from governing bodies over the recent few decades have strengthened this viewpoint since the introduction of legislation such as the 1985 Broadleaf Policy. From this, there still seems to be some perception that conifers are as not as good for wildlife as their 'native' cousins. However, we can see that this is not the case. Conifer forests can support communities of animals that can be found in various habitats around Britain, and also attract their own specialists that are found nowhere else. Britain is a good place to grow trees. The Western edge of our country, from the south west, through Wales and up through to Scotland has the warm and wet conditions suitable for fast-growing conifers, giving high yield timber, on low value agricultural lands. It seems sensible to grow here, as trees grow better, than our continental neighbours. It is perhaps all too easy to forget, that the main reason for the establishment of the New Forests is to supply timber. It just happens that the habitats that the forests create are great for wildlife. The present main management scheme of clearfell lends itself to these wildlife needs, even if they in some areas it needs some adjusting.

Perhaps the public perception has been swayed by nostalgia? Do we see our native woodlands as visions of a Broadleaf Idyll? Wishful thinking perhaps as after all, as Britain is relatively impoverished with its variety of tree compared to its continental neighbours. The various Glacial activities resulting in Britain becoming islands have hampered the recolonization of a richer Broadleaf community. However, since the deforestation of Britain's initial wooded influences over the last two thousand years, to what may be considered to an all-time low of some 5% land cover, any increase should be seen as an improvement for us and its wildlife.

Any large scale conversion to Broadleaf should come under some scrutiny though. Latitude can play its part in choosing whether the planting of these trees for the supposed benefit of wildlife could be justified. For example, any amount of broadleaf planting in the northern parts of our shores or in the uplands (supposing they would grow there in the first place) should be considered. Some key species of animals that perhaps are regarded as vulnerable and could be helped in forest habitat development have limited range within Britain. Woodlark for example, prefers the lower half of Britain, and is on the extreme western edge of its range. Hawfinch, are another broadleaf woodland specialty that are seldom seen at higher latitudes.

The miss-placed stigma that conifers are perceived to be bad for all, is still used in argument by some conservationists today occasionally misleading the general public stating that by acquiring established coniferous woodlands they can be 'saved' by converting them to broadleaf - the benefits that the New Forests bring with what they attract, generally played down in argument.

Although great swathes of land were planted in the first half of the last century leading to major land changes such as in the uplands of north east England, or the Brecklands, a lot of forestry was planted around and on broadleaf influences. Looking on the other side of the coin, here, perhaps some may find the best of both worlds. Birds and animals can integrate between the two types of woodland, where otherwise they may have only favoured one; Wood Warblers and Pied Flycatcher being an example. Perhaps rather than phase out a sensible commercial and wildlife asset such as coniferous woodland in favour for a total broadleaf mindset, a balance is needed?

Green Woodpecker on Anthill

Thicket

The trees that have been planted as saplings between the rows of brash on the clearfell, grow very fast. This can be around 2-3 feet per annum in their first few years, after being spaced about a meter apart. After 4-5 years or so a tangle has developed that becomes difficult to walk through. Although up to perhaps a meter or two high in some places we can just see over the top and to all impressions, it reminds us of a thicket. This mix of branch and invading plant life that struggles between the conifers offers perfect habitat for our scrub and hedgerow bird life.

It is here that Finches and other passerines, or perching birds feed and breed successfully, sometimes in noticeable number. Likewise, it is also a desirable place for mammals such as Deer and Fox to lie up and feel safe.

Whitethroat and Linnet

The edge that is created along the rides and roads that criss-cross the new forests and border thicket-stage forestry offer excellent cover for birds such as Whitethroat and Linnet in which to nest. The former warbler is a migrant to our shores: the latter finch a resident. Both are commonly found within forestry, particularly in lowland Britain. It could be argued that here, where these birds' habitats have come under pressure over the last few decades, and where populations may be under threat elsewhere, the forests could be viewed as havens for.

Whitethroat

Initially, one could say that both the Whitethroat or Linnet are not coniferous birds at all, generally taking a liking to scrubby wasteland and bushy thickets, tangled roadside herbage, or patches of gorse. Compare these areas to what thicket stage forest resembles though, and we can see the connection. Often, structure matters more than particular species of tree or shrub to animals, as long as a food source is available.

Springtime is a great time to look for Whitethroat. Walking along a forest track that is bordered with young conifer, it should not be too long before the bird becomes evident. Its scratchy song standing out, attracting the watcher to see the bird as it perches some six to ten feet up, delivering its angry-sounding oratory.

Likewise the Linnet can also be heard, its song more musical and not so distinct, it soon becoming apparent that the male is usually not on his own, but part of a pair, with the female nearby. In contrast to the Whitethroat, this resident finch is classed as a partial migrant, with some birds leaving our shores for the content during the winter, and others choosing to stay all year round, sometimes forming large flocks living within the forests. Perhaps here the Linnet has an advantage over the Whitethroat, as it can pair up earlier in the year from these flocks, whereas the warbler has to fly from its wintering grounds in the Sahel region of Africa. The visitor then has to attract a mate, but while advertising his presence, he will build a few trial nests for the female to choose from prior to her arrival. On the other hand, with a head start on visitors such as the Whitethroat, resident birds such as the Linnet can generally raise two or three broods in the season, whereas most migrants can only manage one or two.

Further along the track, and another Whitethroat can be heard competing with its neighbour - but at a respectful distance, enough that the birds feel as sufficient to build a nest and find enough food in which to raise a brood.

The Linnet has a slightly different approach than the Whitethroat however. These birds seem to prefer loose colonies or groups. Four or six pairs are not uncommon to nest within close vicinity to each other. Perhaps a product of the flocking behavior of wintertime, they do not find the ability to find food as competitive as other visiting passerines such as warblers.

The nests of the two are similar in structure, being a cup made mostly of grass, with fine roots and hair as a lining. The Linnet may have wool or a few feathers thrown in for good measure. At this time, the Linnet can be quite conspicuous as the pair often fly together; the female collecting nest material and carrying it back to the chosen spot. The male often singing from the nest tree, as the female busily weaves grass or hair into place. Three to four eggs are laid, one each day, from both Linnet and Whitethroat, where incubation starts when the clutch is complete, which is the norm for these small birds. Around twelve days later, the eggs hatch, where both parents feed the young on a variety of insect matter. A week and a half later, the young are ready to leave the nest, but in both cases are still fed by the parents until they become self-sufficient.

At the end of summer, the Whitethroat of course has to head on back to Africa, as its insect and soft fruit diet will eventually run out prior to the oncoming winter.

The Linnet on the other hand switches its diet from insects to seed based matter. Here, it can be seen again along the roads and tracks of the forest feeding on ripened herbage such as Fat hen or Persicaria.

Linnet

Black Grouse

Once widespread across the country some century ago, the Black Grouse, or Blackcock has become marginalized in its distribution, and until recent times could only be found on moorland in upland Britain. Since the establishment of the coniferous forests in these areas, its status is hopefully improving providing the forest in question fulfills certain criteria so the grouse can survive.

This improvement arguably is largely due to a realization of how important the commercial forests are, and the implementation of Biodiversity action planning by a number of organizations such as the RSPB, The Game conservancy Trust, and the Forestry Commission itself. Various regional bodies associated with conservation in different parts of the country are also involved, and over the last few years their lot has changed for the better.

A moorland-edge loving bird, it could be described as one which has adapted to the new emerging forests, as the areas that contained them were planted upon. Overgrazing with the introduction of sheep in the uplands has eroded their dietary requirements to the point that open moorland was increasingly becoming unattractive to them. As can be imagined, the heather moorland itself is their established preference, but as long as the woodlands themselves can offer the plant and invertebrate content within them, then the Grouse can live there. It is here where the Biodiversity Action Planning comes in to work. Areas are identified as holding the required plant life such as Heather, Billberry, Clover, and other food plants along with wetter patches which hold the invertebrate life necessary for the young in the breeding season. These are maintained or enhanced by local felling nearby or helped by the creation of wetter areas through stream damming for instance.

However, the woodland also offers necessary seclusion with undisturbed tracts of habitat. Here predator numbers can be controlled – Fox and Crow, and perhaps where too, people in general find access difficult.

Monitoring Black grouse can prove tricky, as the bird generally distributes itself through the forest and adjacent moorland. One way its numbers can be estimated, is through counting the number of breeding males at its annual Lek.

Each year the Male Black Grouse or Blackcock struts his stuff along with others in chosen areas collaborating in a ritualized display, as females look on. Here they sometimes fight in the hope of attracting as many females as they can to mate with and carry on the line. Natural selection in its purist form. Some of these leking areas are years old and can attract many birds, but some can hold as little as half a dozen, and move around almost on a daily basis.

Recent estimates have put the British total of Leking males at about 6500. Compare this with about 25000 in 1990, and we can see that the Black Grouse will need a lot of help if the species is to re-establish its numbers to what are viewed as a healthy level. Hopefully, the upland forests can play their part and ensure that the Black Grouse will remain a part of the British Fauna.

Unoficial Nature Reserves

When walking around a parcel of forestry, it feels like a nature reserve. After all it has its boundaries, so it appears self-contained. Despite its industry, access is freely available. It has an air of a place where nothing else could happen, such as major development. Perhaps it is because we know it is state owned with a stamp of authority - its wardens or foresters policing in a fleet of green and yellow panel vans and 4x4's?

Traveling around the forest along the criss-cross of roads and paths, we come across the various different age-classes within the trees. Where some coupes or areas have been harvested there is bare or open ground. Next door is mature forest. Further over is thicket stage tree growth that has been there for perhaps four or five years or so. All these places providing different structures that a mix of birds and animals find to their liking. It has a regimented air about it which perhaps why some people find it 'too tidy'. Similarly, this exists today with modern farming. Unlike this comparison with agriculture, the ground structure that exists for wildlife to thrive is at a higher level within the forests. The insect and flora that animals depend on, is available. This "pillar"or food chain, that attracts the animals further up is sadly becoming less stable as land is becoming increasingly improved for Agriculture, as has been seen over the past fifty years or so.

Fox

Fallow Deer

The lowland forests of Britain are havens for Fallow Deer. Generally difficult to see at close range, their habits have made them elusive as they shun from human kind. You can see them easily enough in parks and stately homes around Britain because over time they have become used to people, but the forest deer are a completely different animal to watch. Most people are unaware of their presence, mainly because they tend to move about mainly at night, and rest up in areas such as the Pole stage of forestry succession, but you can see them in daylight hours and with a little thought and preparation, they can be further observed or photographed.

A Buck Fallow Deer sniffs the air hoping to catch scent of females nearby in the rut.

Fallow deer live in small groups and prefer each others company, and as a herding animal there is an advantage of being with others to look out for danger. Of course the main beings from man, as there are no big animal predators to feed on them. The main advantage they have over us of course is as with most mammals, is their strong sense of smell. They will discover you long before you will see them, unless, as is sometimes the case, we come across a group from a downwind direction.

In stature, the Fallow Deer is around a meter to its shoulder, is light brown or fawn with lighter spots on its flanks. The Bucks have antlers, which are palmate or spatula shaped,

rather than straight tines or spikes as in the Red Deer. There are colour variations though, and it is not uncommon to see Fallow that are Black, or two tone dark brown and black, and even white. The female or Does lack the antlers as most other deer species do.

The isolated groups composing of single sexed animals move about the forest, foraging on foliage - leaves buds and tree bark as well as similar plants that make up the forest under-story.

Fallow deer are viewed as pests within the forest as they can do damage as shown here within the rut. The tower, or high seat are used by forestry staff to control their numbers.

The rutting stand (below) is a quagmire of mud and urine, churned up by the males.

In the day, they lie up, remaining unobtrusive in forest whether its pole stage in height or the tangle of an established clearfell with its re-growth of Bramble and brash. The groups can move some distance, particularly if the forest is a large one, but generally, they stay within an area of a few square miles if there is sufficient food and solitude.

In some cases, the Fallow deer is viewed as a pest within the forestry industry as it can do a lot of damage trees as they nibble away at small newly planted saplings, or browse on foliage at their own height. To this end, forest rangers regularly try and keep their numbers down, taking out individuals in the winter months with a rifle; such is the number of these animals.

However you look at the Deer situation, the Fallow is another successful addition to enrich our forests. In this light, it is difficult to imagine there could be so many of them living comparatively under most people's noses. Despite controlling methods such as shooting, and exclusion from areas via fencing, the deer are seen as an asset in our fauna.

In the autumn, the groups come together to rut, where the males vie for the attention of the females. Dominant males bellow their loud throaty roar in late September to the end of October, mainly at the early start of the day. An area is chosen where the buck will try and attract as many females as possible and mate when the time is right. These areas are a veritable scene of primeval testosterone, where the ground is ploughed up by the male's hooves. Wet with water and urine, a musky smell permeates the air. Local vegetation is thrashed as the male scrapes his antlers on branch and trunk. Come across such a place, and the animals just melt away, but if observation is the aim, then we need to get off the ground, and take to the trees.

Wildlife rangers have discovered this, and you may come across one of their high seats. Built near open areas within the forest, these deer glades are used as places to control their numbers. They can equally be used to just watch or photograph deer as well of course, but permission is needed before use. It is not only common courtesy, it has safety in mind. After all, it could prevent you from being shot! Another method is to make your own high seat that is convenient for both yourself and of course the deer, after you locate a rutting group. These rutting sites are usually used year after year, so with forward planning, a high seat could be built out-of-season in advance.

After the rigors and hopefully entertainment of the rutting season, the single fawn is born the following spring, in late May or July, staying with the female groups and in the case of bucks, probably the following year before joining their all male clubs.

Groups of Fallow Deer Are usually same-sexed, in this case containing young as well as females.

Other Species

It is not only the Fallow Deer that has taken advantage of the haven that the New Forests offer. Species such as Muntjac and Sika have also found plantations to their liking. Chinese Water Deer have likewise become established after they were introduced in small numbers over the past fifty years or so, forming some 10% of the worlds' population here. Most of these species have seen gradual increases in the Southern parts of Britain over the past few decades after escaping from deer parks or private collections. Wild Boar is another large mammal that is expanding its range after escaping from farms. The Forest of Dean and nearby Welsh forests showing increased activity from this new inclusion to our countryside.

WATER

Water is an important resource for the growth of vegetation throughout its development. Some trees however are not as generally dependant on water as others. Hence there are some Pines which prefer the dryer soils such as in the east, or the sandier coasts of Wales, but on the other hand Spruces can tolerate a higher level of rainfall in western districts and the north, for example.

In any woodland type however, water is an essential requirement to the animals that live within them. Water courses, such as streams, ponds, lakes or lochs, may have been already established prior to the creation of the forests, but in the early days of woodland development, they were not given much consideration and were perhaps seen as an unnecessary break in forest creation. Planting was carried out right up to the water's edge in those days, which would eventually shade out any riparian herbage and as a result, water loving birds such as Dipper and Grey Wagtail would move on. Part of the problem here also, was the realisation of acids building up in the water; a process which could deplete nutrients and insect life, and have a knock-on effect to bird life and mammals such as Otters.

A complex issue, as initially the effect was solely blamed on conifers themselves. However, this is only part of the story, as the underlying rock and soil compositions contribute, with some broadleaf trees having also been realised as contributors.

It has also been found, that conifers have an ability in to filtering out sulphates and other pollutants from the air, so perhaps this has been a contributing factor.

A male Goldeneye displays on a Loch within forestry in Scotland. A variety of waterbirds find such places within commercial forests in which to live, at some stage in their lives.

It seems that Britain with its mainly prevalent south-westerly winds, is not so effected as their continental neighbours, as our pollutants drift their way. Lowering of atmospheric pollutants in general, of course would seem to be a way of overcoming these issues.

The aspect of acid rain has been a worry to environmentalists for some time, and studies of Dippers have identified that conifers as a dominating part of the stream-side have a detrimental effect on their breeding performance, so any restructuring by opening up streams and rivers is seen as a practical improvement.

Birds such as Dippers suffer badly when trees are planted up to the waters' edge. Opening up these riparian areas can only help their return.

These hydrology protection zones are becoming policy, and create riparian areas for other animals such as Grey Wagtail and insect life such as Damselfly. On a physical and mechanical aspect, tree harvesting and thinning practices were also detrimental to watercourses in the past, as they were frequently used as unofficial roadways for tractors and other machinery. Any such physical activity along with this type of ground disturbance, could as imagined, have far reaching impact outside the forest area, downstream.

Drainage was seen as essential in the forests make-up in the early days. The result was extensive build-up of silt in any waterway that it would eventually find its way into. Streams and smaller rivers, after time, became clogged with this run-off, particularly after the churning effect that mechanisation had during harvesting, for example. The policy of using streams as unofficial roadways, has now thankfully stopped.

Trees were also planted on any damp areas that were deemed to be of use, often to their detriment, as the wet conditions were unsuitable for them, often holding back growth. In the long-term here, any monitory return was low from planting in such areas, with the whole process becoming uneconomical when harvesting came to fruition.

The creation of waterways within the forests sometimes bring surprises.
Water Rails are not ususally assosiated with such habitat, but frequently use these places in winter.
Here the bird hunts for Frogletts and Newts.

Thankfully, attitudes have changed, with more consideration given to what watercourses and ponds have to offer in providing a diverse flora and fauna. Increased knowledge and experience has also taught that these places are best avoided in the planting regime. Generally, now streams are being opened up from encroaching trees, with more daylight being allowed to enter, encouraging plants to flourish which of course then attracts birds and animals.

Greylag Goose.

It has also been realised that the inclusion of broadleaf trees along streams during this second phase in forestry brings increased diversity amongst the forest. With such an opportunity to improve, the creation of shaded and open areas can make a difference for fish, for example. Here again, insect life is promoted, with the residual leaf litter breaking down quicker than its coniferous counterparts.

Its Raining

When rain has occurred, puddles are formed in ditches and tyre tracks. Marshy places are replenished, which are then used by animals such as birds to drink and bathe; in some cases vital particularly if they (and we) want them to stay.
With these oases having being created, they may encourage animals that use these features as their primary habitats, such as amphibians, and thus increase the mix of inhabitants within the forest boundary that perhaps were not there before.

Pond creation is an important tool with which the Wildlife Ranger can bring diversity
to the forest. Their establishment bringing almost instantanious results.

Over- Uath Lochans, Speyside, Highlands.
Used by Goldeneye and Divers for breeding.

A lot of the bird life found within the forest is of the seed-eating variety, and they drink regularly throughout their day. On fine days, and in times of water shortage, ponds and streams are the more important to Crossbills, Siskin and Goldfinch for example, and large concentrations of these types of birds can be seen using them. They offer a splash of colour if lucky enough to be seen. Reds, Yellows and Emeralds; an exotic addition to our avifauna. Residents that perhaps most people do not realise are native, and are not from some far-away jungle.

Honey-pots for birds, insects and other animals, Foresters value the significance of water supplies, and pond creation is an important tool in increasing overall diversity. At local levels, rangers can see an area that could benefit. Perhaps only a single species may be the initial driving force in the creation or refurbishment of these water features, but helping other species in the process. At this local level, any form of this direct conservation can deliver positive results that are almost immediately visible. By creating such places for birds and other animals to use, another amenity is created for us, to be able to enjoy them.

Of course, these actions are not the primary concern of the foresters. Growing trees are. However changing attitudes allow this element of expenditure to happen within the forest infrastructure. Pond creation increases biodiversity in a forest, and is a major conservation aim. Particularly in areas such as Pine woodlands, which are often established on dry, sandy soils which generally lack water features compared with other wetter coniferous woodlands.

Amphibians that make use of pond or marsh are good indicators of water quality. Frogs and newts taking advantage of situations that are already available or are created can make a big difference to overall populations of these types of animal, because outside the forest these areas are often used for other reasons rather than for wildlife to live in. Insect life is dramatically increased with the inclusion of water. Water Bugs and damselfly for example, forming part of a make-up of insect life that live in and around, then spreading into the forest proper. All diversify the food chain that exists, each increasing the prospect for others whether they are Dragonflies which prey on insects themselves, or for the birds and animals that prey on them.

In some areas, where water is formed in major bodies, such as Lochs or lakes, they may attract species that are special to them. Some types of wildfowl may have already being using them since the forest was added, and then there are those situations that can be managed to suit particular species

In Scotland, for example, rare breeding birds such as Goldeneye are encouraged to use some of the lochs within the forest.

Lack of holes in trees is generally a problem for them, so nest boxes have seen to be the answer. Divers can also be provided for, as floating pontoons are constructed for them to nest on. These are some of the rarest and sensitive of British breeding birds, and any increase of their status can only be a plus point.

Bringing major benefits to the forest, water courses play a major part in the aesthetic make-up for those who just wish to enjoy the forests as a space. Calming to the nature lover, and if large enough, some even useful for water-loving sports. It is a big part of a vision by governments, of how we may all benefit from the forest as a resource. Forests have an aspect to absorb people interest where open space such as Farmland seem to lack such ability. And still there are some forests that are so large and remote, they can house sensitive animal life.

Dragonfly

POLE STAGE

The trees are above three meters in height, and, if we are looking at Spruce, then there is little or no foliage layer beneath the canopy. It has been blotted out. Each tree touches its neighbour and our view is of a line of trunks, or a wall of conifer needles. Almost an impenetrable barrier, it asks the question whether anything could live within it at all? If we are determined,we could perhaps force our way through to the dead lower branches into a quiet, almost sterile world.

Initially, apart from the occasional path that exists through it, as a result of thinning, it could be a long walk before one reaches 'the other side'. This then, is mainly of use only to those who can live within the top canopy, or can make their way through any gaps that do exist, perhaps to use as shelter.

Pole stage is probably the first stage in tree husbandry, as the wood needs thinning out, and lower branches trimmed. Some of the timber is ideal for fence posts and other similar sized items. This initial harvesting in turn gives remaining trees more room to develop growth, as they increase in height and girth. With the creation of another type of habitat, allowing some ground flora to develop in the case of Larch or Scots Pine, for example, other birds and animal species find a niche in which to live in. This process of brashing, or removal of the lower branches is vital for light to reach the floor, if ground herbage is preferred, which is generally more beneficial in attracting wildlife within these less dense conifers.

This period of the forests succession could be argued as least attractive to wildlife, but as with any situation, there are those who take advantage.

Goldcrest

Being Britain's smallest bird, the Goldcrest can be found in conifer woodlands up and down the country at all times of the year. It especially resides within the forests, particularly liking to work the canopy of pole stage and mature conifer plantations looking for food items. However, it can also be found outside the forest enclave in parks and gardens and mixed woods, probably spreading from nearby conifer woodlands.

Being a small bird, it looks for insect items that live within the trees. Small spiders and beetles for example, live year round whether at the adult stage, or as their larvae, enough even in winter months.

Its musical repetitive "deedle-dee" song can be a giveaway of its presence as it flits within the fronds and needles. Probably only found in a few localities in the last century, the Goldcrest has spread as the commercial forests have been created across the British Isles. This diminutive, forever-busy bird can be seen at various heights in the canopy, and can be quite approachable, but still better viewed through binoculars. After all, it does weigh less than a 10 pence coin!

Its noticeable feature, as its name implies, is its golden yellow stripe or crown, which is occasionally extended perhaps when other birds of its kind are near. It's intent a form of communication and display.

Up to a dozen eggs can be laid into the small nest, which is often slung under an outward frond.

Like most birds, the Goldcrest breeds in the spring, with the male attracting a female with its song. A nest is built, a three layer cup, consisting of moss, small twigs and a cobweb and feather lining. With its internal dimensions around three inches, it is supported under a branch by more cobwebs. Amazingly, nine to eleven eggs are laid within, a strategy that mirrors other small birds such as tits, as losses in the initial bird's lives are many with predation playing a part with most that have these high clutch levels. A second batch of eggs are sometimes started elsewhere before the first leave, with the male getting most of the work done regarding nest construction, as the female tends the first brood. The incubation period is some 16 to 19 days.

For the Goldcrest, the future looks good thanks to the establishment of the New Forests. It does suffer in times of severe winters however, as do a lot of small birds when the population is hit hard and many perish, but they usually bounce back when winter weather ameliorates over a period of years.

Studies Within The Forests

The New Forests had generally been overlooked in terms of bird study in the first fifty years of their existence. There is early work though, by ornithologists such as the Lacks, in the thirties and Moss and Bibby in the seventies and eighties, pointing the way in which birds inhabit the new forests at various times in the trees development. From the Commissions conception, and of course, since the time forests have matured and been replaced, ornithologists have discovered a pattern which generally repeats itself regarding bird life in the woodlands.

As each successive stage develops, from whether it is newly planted trees on virgin ground, or to mature forest, a different community of birds reside, with the general successive stage giving greater diversity. Also, this make-up of the different bird communities' changes as tree structure develops. For example, at the thicket stage, small passerines such as Whitethroat or Willow warbler find this habitat to their liking. However, when the forest canopy closes in the next say ten years, then these birds move to other areas and different species find it suitable. Goldcrest, Chaffinch and Sparrowhawk, being notable.

Studies have also shown that restock forests hold a more diverse community than newly planted lands. This is probably borne out by the fact that recently harvested coupes have birds which are relatively nearby compared to say an isolated moorland. From this then, we can see that a checkered or patchwork of successive stages as the forest develops helps the colonization of newly created habitat and increases the total number of species overall in the whole forest.

Willow Warbler

As far as numbers are concerned, it is impossible to say with certainty just how many of a particular species of birds exist. The British Trust for Ornithology, which co-ordinates nationwide counts, does so from volunteer involvement and cannot cover the whole of the country. Particularly remote and often least-visited upland forests for example may get little attention. It does however give an indication, and can give trends for what we can expect, and where estimates can be predicted.

Mammals are another case in point. Being not as visible as birds, their numbers perhaps can only be guessed upon. With widely fluctuating populations, in some cases, where expansion and contraction regularly play a part in their numbers and hence distribution, smaller mammal numbers can only be imagined. Creation of habitat such as forestry, conservative agriculture practices and better education against persecution hopefully can improve their lot. Perhaps animals such as Polecat or Stoat perhaps will then become more noticeable within the countryside.

Numbers of small mammals within the forests, such as Stoat can only be imagined as they are secretive and not generally noticeable.

Larger Mammal populations are also intriguing. It was for a long time assumed that Red Deer were just inhabitants of the high tops and open moorland. However it has become realized that significant populations are living within the forests. These, and other deer's expansion aided by the commercial forests around the country.

It seams that an element of confrontation had been created between conservationists and foresters. With this initial climate that the former was geared up to the opposition of forestry and its expansion, it is no wonder that any positive outlook or value existed for the habitat at all. A situation that still exists in some minds today.

Some animals such as the Red Grouse have an obvious monetory value, as in their case through shooting interests. But what of Goshawk orChaffinch?

With the climate of mistrust between foresters and conservationists, any serious study seemed to be looked at with a negative outlook, and it was some time before general interest was focused on the coniferous enclave once again.

However not all conservationists saw it this way. True, the more hard-nosed saw the establishment of the plantations as a disaster as far as any wildlife was concerned. In this light though, a few saw the potential that the forests had.

Wide-scale planting can obviously be detrimental to birds such as the rarer waders as in the case of the flow country, but it made some look at forestry, and indeed moorland with a more critical eye.

Two such scientists, Mark Avery and Roderick Leslie published a book in the late eighties*(Birds and Forestry, Poyser)* in response to this, and painted a picture of how we could see forestry in terms of wildlife habitat, posing the question as to what value in terms of wildlife has forestry to offer. They also looked at reasons why we should look at moorland and identify which areas were significant, which could be protected, and other open areas which were not so productive for these 'special' birds. These ideas could then be used when future forest expansion proposals develop.

Important questions were highlighted. For example, how can we put a value on certain wildlife? If we talk about game birds such as in the case of Grouse shooting for example, then an obvious monitory value may be calculated. It may be difficult though to actually put a value on Goshawks or Chaffinch, apart from a rarity value or in biomass comparisons. But what about the value that we put on wild creatures for just being what they are? In many people's eyes of course, this is priceless.

It was interesting that Avery and Leslie pointed out that the commoner birds found in the New forests should not be discarded being of no value. In fact a study by Moss found that there were significantly more songbirds found in Sitka plantations (southern Scotland) than some farmland found in the south of Britain.

It remained the case that the true or total value could not be put on the amount of bird life that exists within our commercial forests. At least the more familiar, or commoner species anyway. More work needs to be done to assess biomass and overall population densities in comparison to their other habitats. Take a woodland winter ramble in lowland Britain however, and it becomes immediate that these birds play a big part in inhabiting commercial forestry.

Long Eared Owl

Britain's most nocturnal of Owls, the Long Eared, could be the most overlooked. Everyone is familiar with the "twoo-wit, twoo-woo" of the Tawny, which is found throughout most parts of Britain in its parks, woods and gardens, but its cousin the Long Eared, with its quieter, low hoot is a little more difficult to find. It is a bird primarily of the conifer woods, particularly of upland country. Here, because woodland is seldom visited, even by those interested in birds, their populations are probably very much underestimated.

In years past though, the bird was a common breeder over much of Britain where early farming methods were a help in supplying its staple food of rodents. In the east of Britain, it could be found in copses and deciduous woodlands.

The attraction of the forests to the owls of course is the dense foliage, along with the seclusion they offer, but they are also attracted to land that is adjacent to open ground such as moorland. Like the Merlin, which can also nest in the conifers that are a part of upland Britain today, the owls glean most of their food from these open areas, and which are an integral part of their survival.

Long Eared Owls nest in structures that are already provided for them. Old Crow, Wood pigeon nests, or a squirrel drey are favoured places in which to lay their 3-5 white, rather round-shaped eggs.

On occasions, where there is no structure to use, then they will nest on the ground. This has its negative points because it is easier for predators such as Fox to discover them. The bird has also taken to use baskets that have been provided by sympathetic birders, an extension of the popular nest box idea that we use in our gardens.

Seldom seen in the wild, the young can give their presence away, and it is not uncommon to see the offspring perched on the outer edge of the conifer forest in daylight hours. It is thought there could be between 1100 and 3600 pairs within Britain, but due to its illusive nature and the fact that so much coniferous forest is not monitored, it is unsure to be specific in numbers. It has a green status within the conservation ranking system for Britain. In winter, the population is bolstered by birds from Fennoscandia, where they can be occasionally found in coastal regions, and generally is easier to see.

The most nocturnal of Owls, the Long Eared is often amongst forestry that borders upland moorland. Here they can find the seclusion and the food they need.

Sparrowhawk

Although the Sparrowhawk can be found in a lot of habitats that have a wooded theme, they show a preference for nesting in conifers. A true woodland bird, its colouration has a divergent link with others of its kind. Horizontally-barred patterning on its breast helps in to brake up its form as it hides in undergrowth, while a slate blue back in the case of the male is a standard colouration of a bird hunter, reflected by others such as Peregrine falcon and Merlin. All are high speed operators.

This small dashing hawk can sometimes be mistaken for the Kestrel, but its fast and low flight, along with short rounded wings clearly mark it apart from the hovering falcon. The Sparrowhawk has also the reputation as having the biggest size difference between male and female, more than any other bird of prey. The latter being almost twice the size of her opposite. This size difference, influencing how the two live.

In nesting preferences, it shows a clear favour for trees that are spaced from two to four meters apart. Any closer together or further apart are generally unused to build its nest. Late pole stage of six to ten meters high, trees that have had an initial thinning, are perfect to their needs. It prefers to use a specific site each year, with a new nest constructed each time, so a collection of past nests are usually around the site.

In the nesting period, whether while the female is incubating, or later when she joins the Male in supplying food items for the growing brood, the two generally operate collecting prey in two different areas. The smaller Male prefers to hunt within the tangle of forest itself, generally in the vicinity of the nest. The female however prefers to range a little further away, sometimes braking from the forest and entering surrounding farmland.

Because of the striking difference in size, the two can spread their preferences in prey items. The Male will take birds up to the size of the larger thrushes, while the female can take bigger fayre such as Woodpigeon.

The population has more female birds than males, and because the latter has a tendency to range over a larger area, when it comes to nesting time, the males come into more contact with prospective mates.

For her part, the female is looking for a successful provider, so at the time of laying, incubation and raising the nestlings, she has to be sure that the male is up to supplying enough food. At egg development, she cannot be too involved in hunting, as her weight is at its maximum, and possible injury to herself and any developing eggs may occur. This reliance of the male, and the ability of the surrounding area in providing food, is key to whether breeding is successful in terms of the number of young that are raised to disperse, and carry on the parental legacy.

The two birds both construct a nest, usually using conifer branches, Larch being a favourite as the nodes along the length help to interlock the structure. Three to six eggs are laid, cryptically coloured, with a pale blue background. Red and brown blotches then lend the eggs an element of camouflage when the female sees it necessary to leave the nesting area, perhaps to repel a predator.

The female alone incubates, and they hatch asynchronously after around 33 days. This mechanism is thought to guard against the hard times, if food is in short supply, so the younger perish to safeguard at least some of the birds getting to the fledgling stage.

The development of the young is interesting in that although the females gain weight faster, feather and behavioural development in the males is quicker. In this way, they can compete for food with their bigger sisters. They are also the first to fly, some four days before.

For the following three or four weeks the fledglings stay in the vicinity of the nest, where then both parents can supply the necessary food for their further development. Here too, they can hone the flying and hunting skills they need to help them live independently. After this period, the young travel their own separate ways. Dispersing in the August and September, they are never too far away, the usual distance being within 20km, eventually, finding a niche in which to live in.

Looking at population coverage of the Sparrowhawk, they show an even distribution across the British Isles, with the major concentration of birds living at lower elevations where they are generally more successful. Being one of our most common birds of prey, they can be found wherever there are birds to be caught, with only the highest altitudes that have no suitable nesting habitat and hence fewer birds. The problem of pesticides in agriculture, which had such an impact on hunters such as the Sparrowhawk in the 1950's has now passed, and the numbers of these and other raptors has recovered and increased. Generally, the bird can also be found outside the areas of conifer woodlands and are common in town parks and gardens showing that they can adapt to other habitats as long as there is a food source available in small birds.

The Edge Effect

Studies have been carried out regarding the effects on how the forests around our uplands impact on bird and other animal that live within its immediate vicinity. Some open-loving birds obviously will no doubt be displaced when forests grow to canopy closure. The Edge of a forest will also for example have a physical presence that will dissuade some birds from living in close proximity to the tree line. For instance, it is fair to argue that perhaps the forest could harbor higher levels of predation through Crow and Fox inhabiting the wooded enclaves that may have not otherwise been there. Whinchat as mentioned previously, are another case where they have been shown to suffer from avian predation, if choosing to live near the forest boundary.

Vegetation may also be altered by the nearby tree growth. Land regime changes such as heather management (rotational burning for shooting interests), may be abandoned, and grazing routines may change, altering the floral make up of the area.

These aspects should of course influence where future forests should lay, and the best sites for our rarer upland inhabitants be safeguarded beforehand, but on the other side of the coin, we should realize that other communities of birds and animals that the forests bring, will prosper. Each species has its own requirements for living. As we have seen, some will take advantage of the newly planted areas for a while, while others can fit in with the concept of commercial forestry provided some criteria are evident.

The Merlin is a good example. Seen as an open loving bird, it feeds on small birds such as the Meadow Pipit, and moorland is its preferred habitat. Mainly a ground-nester, it will raise a family in heather or other rank herbage. As well as this situation, it will also take to using old Crows' nests either in isolated trees, or as found to be the case, along the edge of the nearby conifer forests.

In Northumberland, for example, it has been established they have a higher breeding success than ground-nesting pairs, possibly due to less predation or unintentional disturbance. Although blanket forestry of large tracts of land has displaced some Merlin territories, it seems that the population may stabilize in these areas providing that there is enough open land adjacent to existing forest for the bird in which to hunt.

Study by the Hawk and Owl trust also showed that re-structuring the forest helps the situation for Merlin. Although it is no substitute for the moorland loving bird, it can help by providing areas to supplement its hunting territory by providing open aspects within the forest.

Merlin sometimes use forestry in which to nest and take advantage of the protection it has to offer by getting up off the ground. It is still dependent on open moorland in which to hunt however.

Coal Tit

The Coal Tit is one of the most common inhabitants of the conifer forest. However it can also be found in parks and gardens, attracted to exotic conifers which have been planted more for their ornamental aspects than any benefit for animals themselves. Overall, the new commercial forests have only bolstered a population that had already been widespread, with records noting that even since the 1800's, they have been numerous. Noticeably, the tit is more widespread than any other in the upland forests, and could be the most commonly found bird within established, older forestry. At all locations, it is often seen along with other tits in the winter months, travelling in groups around the woodlands in search of food.

The Coal Tit, like others of its kind, is a hole-nester. Rotten wood, cavities in walls, and where no such situations for them exist, even holes found in the ground. This can be common in the new plantations, where the lack of rotten wood is prevalent due to a healthy tree stock. However in mixed woodlands such as in lowland Britain, there are usually places in which to nest within any deciduous influences.

It is usual to find members of the tit family paired up, each accompanying the other as they inquisitively investigate any nook and cranny in their busy lives. Always in vocal contact, they have a collection of whistles and 'chips' which remind its mate where the other is, and alerts us to their presence.

As with that other small bird, the Goldcrest, it is adept at feeding in conifer needles, where its small size, fine bill and acrobatic skill, is perfect for finding small insect matter.

When it does come to nesting, perhaps ten eggs may be laid in the nest of hair, spiders' webs, and feathers, fashioned in a loose cup, reminiscent of other hole-nesting tits.

The Coal Tit is another small bird that benefits from feeding on insects that live within the conifers needles.

The status of the Coal Tit is a good one, where apart from the odd cold winter, which seem to take its toll on any small bird of its size, it is nowhere under threat as a species. Indeed some common bird census findings with the BTO can put some populations of up to 100 pairs /km in thicket stage conifers, but the usual is about 12 in other habitats. Estimates put their numbers of almost a million pairs in Britain and Ireland.

Roads and Paths: Open spaces.

The roads and paths that serve as access to the forests can benefit wildlife in various ways. One main aspect is that they break up the regimental aspect of trees. Continuous, even-aged conifers may be locked into a block that may not have any natural break, and may run for quite some distance before the stand finds an open area.

Spotted Flycatcher

This situation then, creates edge. This type of edge effect is created when any part of the forest is for one reason or another is interrupted. Windthrow (trees that have been prematurely blown down), re-structuring, the installation of Deer rides, or harvesting are usual examples of how this is created, but paths and rides create permanent edge.

It is this woodland edge created by roads and pathways within the forest that can be so attractive to some birds and animals. The light availability, along with little or no herbicide use provides ideal conditions in which plants can thrive. Creating opportunity for plants to gain a foothold where normally outside the forest in field margins, for example, they would normally be cut or dressed.

There are some birds in particular that use this woodland edge in various ways. Spotted Flycatchers find the outside branches to their liking, and hawk into open space for their flying insect food. Nightjars operate in a similar manner. Buzzard, Capercaillie and Goshawk use path and road as fly ways. Willow warbler, which is one of the most common species found within the forest, frequently prefers to nest beside paths, and birds such as Chaffinch find the edge useful as song posts - good places to show off to others of their kind.

Roadside verges and paths within the forest harbour a variety of plant-life such as Foxglove. Some others are valuable food sources to insects such as the migrant Painted Lady(above right) or, when deciduous influences are apparent, White Admiral Butterflies.

Natural regeneration can also take a hold along roads and paths, and it is not uncommon to see the established native stand repeating itself roadside, an aspect which is particularly noticeable within upland forests.

Wind distributors such as Rosebay Willow Herb and Thistle attract seed-eating birds that reside. Goldfinch, Linnet and Siskin find that roadside seed-bearing plants supply much needed food in the autumn and winter. In lowland forestry, particularly in the summer months when herbage has had time to grow, it becomes evident that numerous plant species are established.

The Forester also finds that the herbaceous content that is found along these arteries of forest particularly useful to insects such as Butterflies. Much has been done to increase the diversity of the plant communities through modelling roadside edges. For example, cutting regimes are rescheduled in areas that forest rangers find that insects could be encouraged by suitable food plants, and scalloped edges are installed to create 'pockets' in the hope of encouraging areas for plant development.

Juvenile Goldfinch.

Mature Forestry

The coniferous forest is now perhaps fifty years or more in age, and the canopy has attained its full height and development. How long it stays this way depends on what level of demand for its wood is at the time, and how the foresters view what people and wildlife see in its attraction at that particular site. It should be noted of course, that it is part of an industry, with the production of timber the main priority, and there comes a time when the wood will be harvested. This in turn will create another habitat – clearfell, and the cycle is complete.

Nevertheless, felling can be brought forward, or delayed for reasons such as wildlife or an amenity interest, or being part of a restructuring programme. Coniferous trees lack the deep-rooted structure of Broadleaf trees, and are susceptible to wind damage. This Windthrow has a significant impact on the mature tree, and how long it is safe to stand, so in some cases it is beneficial to fell early.

Particularly attractive to active sports enthusiasts - some welcome such as mountain biking and walkers, others not so as in the case of unsupervised motorbike scrambling for instance, foresters and wildlife rangers accommodate the various tastes in leisure and try to balance them with the interests of wildlife.

With these aspirations and demands of use by different parties, the FC has had its fair share of criticism over the last 90-odd years and from time to time has had to endure some bad press. But isn't this to be expected with any large nationally run government body? In hindsight, it is fair to say that mistakes have been made in the past with general policies, and local decisions regarding specific sites, but it also should be noted that it has provided positive ways of both providing a sustainable supply of timber for us all to use and is helping our wildlife. Attitudes can sway policy and thought of how bodies could be managed, and improvements are inevitable. There will always be critics that have valid points of view of how the forests should be managed, and we should applaud this, because it is input that is needed to implement better measures.

On the flip side to this of course, is that the commission has had its fair share of good press. People in general have high regard for our forests, even if more than 50% of them are made up of which some call alien conifers. This was crystallized when the recent government proposition was dropped to its mass sell-off in 2010. The general outcry that Forestry took on in the 1980s over planting in the uplands was forgotten in the 2000s. We suddenly realised how precious our state-owned forests had become.

Since its formation, the Commission has promoted private enterprise in establishing forestry around Britain, and this now occupies more than 40% of the commercial forests in total. Naturally, politicians' have major influence on any government body in how it operates, and the Forest industry is no exception.

For decades, the FC has supplied timber for our needs irrespective of the current climate politically, but this may radically change over the next few years. Some see the recent proposals to amalgamate the various FC bodies with other agencies (such as the environment agency and CCW in Wales) as disaster for our tree growing industries. Certainly the way we grow our timber may influence the overall mix of birds and animals we can find there today, and changes in husbandry could result in the forests animal make-up in the future. Others see it as a 'back door' way of selling of our national asset to fund other projects such as flood defence, for example. Forestry has always been controversial!

Goshawk

The Goshawk can best be described as one of the newest birds of the commercial forest.
This is because it has only begun to thrive here in the latter part of the twentieth century,
due to persecution in Britain. In fact it was for the most part extinct as a breeding bird,

and reintroduced back into the habitat it prefers - the coniferous enclave. It has had a meteoric rise since its reintroduction, and has become the top woodland avian predator in Britain.

The nearest common bird to compare it with in size is the Buzzard, which most people are familiar with. In reality, it is a little larger, with the Goshawk being heavier. As females within bird of prey are bigger than their male counterparts in any case, a female Goshawk weighs in at half a kilo more than a female Buzzard. But apart from its size, what other reasons have helped the Goshawk to become so successful?

One primary factor is that it has taken advantage of forests that are sometimes remote, mostly undisturbed, and rich in food. Due to a secretive nature, it can hide within the trees and is difficult to see. Here they can find sanctuary.

For the Goshawk, Its breeding behaviour has also helped its spread. Generally, raptors of this size do not become ready to breed in until their second year, but studies have revealed that Goshawk can, and do breed in their first adult year, although they are more successful as they get older. In places such as Wales, the bird has become fairly widespread as the amount of forest there has matured, and has provided the perfect environment for it to flourish. Some of these wooded areas are even close to towns and villages where for the most part its inhabitants are blissfully unaware of their presence.

How has the Goshawk earned the right to become the top avian bird of prey within the commercial forest? This has come about because at one time or another most other avian hunters save for the Eagle and perhaps the Peregrine, have ended up on its menu, albeit in very small numbers. It is of course much bigger than its cousin the Sparrowhawk, and because of this prefers to eat bigger food items. A study has revealed in the main however, it prefers to eat birds and mammals that are prevailant in or near to its surroundings. For example, in the deeper forests it may prefer to eat mostly members of the Crow family, Squirrel, or Thrush, but on the edge of a wood high up on moorland, it may prefer Grouse, occasionally Rabbit or Whinchat for example.

Spring is a good time to start to try and see Goshawk. Looking above the tree canopy on a fine day may be rewarding with birds in display. The males purposely circle around high up with deliberate drawn out wing beats.

This cements the fact that a territory exists here to other Goshawks. In the breeding season, you may also come across a breeding pair near to a path within their woodland. They will soon let you know as the loud staccato " kek kek kek" calls warn you that you must keep away. At other times, it is possible to come across the birds perched on the woodland edge or flying through the canopy as it goes about its general day to day activity.

Breeding

For the Goshawk, its breeding year may start as early as February or March, when the two birds who (if they have survived the rigours of the winter months) have stayed together. In some cases though, one of the pair may leave or has died and its opposite joined by a new individual.

The nesting area is a traditional site and the same nest may be used year in year out, but occasionally a new nest may be built nearby, if the old one is not repaired. They are fiercely territorial, as after all they rely on the immediate area as a food source. You will find that the Goshawk prefers the mature forest, when the forester has taken out the close-growing trees after a course of thinning, and perhaps there are three or four meters between each tree. They like Larch, but will use Spruce, even well grown mature Douglas fir. The nest itself is usually near the top of the canopy, close to the main trunk, perhaps forty feet up.

The platform of twigs and stick is lined with spruce, larch branches or fronds. Usually with a shallow cup being around 80-120cm in diameter when newly made, it can increase enormously, with some examples weighing up to a ton when refurbished year on year. About a month is set aside in its construction, but can be as little as eight days if one is repaired after being blown out with inclement weather.

Female Goshawks stay with the young for a few weeks after they hatch, protecting them from predators and inclement weather and feeding them with food brought in by the male.

The bird, as far as reproduction is concerned, is quite predictable. The average laying date in Wales is mid April, with each egg being laid on two or three day intervals, usually with 2-3 eggs. Incubated by the female, it will be another 35 days before the fluffy white chicks can be fed, when incubation is complete. Initially, the female spends the first two weeks of this time with the small young, brooding in inclement weather, offering protection, and feeding them with food items brought in by the male.

Food is passed to the female by its mate who advertises his return with a call, and generally passes it to her away from the nest. Occasionally, the male will bring in prey items, but this tends to be later, when the female joins in hunting for food. The young will spend some six weeks in the nest as they grow from small white down-clad chicks into something which resembles the powerful looking adult.

When the chicks have finally left the nest, they can be quite entertaining as they strengthen their flying skills. Vocal, they can easily be located in what has become a quiet time in the forest, as the majority of the smaller singing birds become less vociferous and

concentrate on bringing up their families, with no immediate need to advertise their presence. Young Goshawk on the other hand can be anything but quiet. Their calls are different from those of young buzzard. The call is more laboured and "wheezy",

The white downy chicks eventually grow into the cinnamon coloured birds which resemble the adult.

increasing in fervour as the chicks fly around, sometimes together, never far away but generally still in the vicinity of the nesting site. They can be quite approachable, but the best method is to sit still nearby, perhaps creeping up to get a better view. The adults themselves can be seen at this time too, as they bring food back, and seemingly forcing the young to chase them for what offerings they have. Perhaps this is a way of teaching them to catch their own, or helping to improve their flying skills?

Larch is a favourite nesting tree. The nodes along the branches length help the twigs to hold the nest structure together.

Now looking more the part of the top avian hunter, the youngsters can be tempted down to feed on nature watchers' offerings such as a rabbit road-kill. The young birds spend a further 50 days or so with their parents honing these skills.

Apart from its springtime display, it is true that the most likely sights are of birds are of those that may be hunting. The characteristic low glide as it speeds through a forest clearing in the hope of catching unwitting prey, travelling from one favoured perch to another. They are however protected by law against disturbance at their nest site, and a special licence is needed if one wishes to study or photograph them, but later on as older birds in late summer, they can be approached.

As far as distribution is concerned, it can be found at random around the British Isles, with numbers increasing as the forests mature. The future looks bright for the Goshawk, as it becomes further established, but there are areas that should contain more. Persecution, from Game keeping and pigeon fanciers, for example, has kept the bird from increasing from Scotland and the North of England. Here and in other areas where shooting interests are popular, the habit of young birds taking a liking for young pheasants in rearing pens have not helped, as they can be easily be shot, even though it is illegal - a situation that existed for some time in the East of the country.

In falconry circles, the Goshawk is highly prized. Its design as a flying hunter dictates that it is better suited to operating in woodland, compared to falcons, which are open ground hunters. The illegal trade in birds of prey was a problem particularly for birds such as the Peregrine Falcon in the past, as birds were stolen from the wild and sold on for large sums of money. A similar situation existed with the Goshawk.

DNA profiling has helped in closing the trade, as birds lineage can be easily tracked, so hopefully the practice is not so much of a problem, along with egg collecting for birds of prey such as these. The fact that they are increasing in numbers obviously helps. Interestingly, it may have been falconers that had have been mainly instrumental in the Goshawk gaining a toehold in the British Isles in the early 1970s, through direct release.

This meteoric rise of the Goshawk is largely due to the creation of the New Forests providing ideal habitat. With this situation existing, have the forest-owning bodies any responsibilities? The fact is, the commission takes the view of wildlife management very seriously, and measures are taken to safeguard Goshawk welfare. The Goshawk has been extensively researched over the past 50 years or so, both here and on the continent and through these studies, some measures have been realised. For example, if general harvesting is scheduled around the breeding period, and kept some 400 meters away, this will give the birds some breathing space and a little solitude. As the birds are site specific, there is usually another stand for them to use nearby, and they can and do switch to these.

As can be appreciated, some of the commercial forests of Britain are of considerable size, and not all can effectively be monitored. Since the first breeding record in 1968, the numbers have increased. In 1994, the British population was numbered at around 400 pairs, but experts thought it more likely to be 600 to 800 pairs. It seems that these numbers are set to increase year on year with saturation point reaching the larger forests before the birds make use of smaller parcels of woodland, and perhaps semi-urban situations.

As fledglings, young birds sit about the vicinity of the nest, waiting for their parents to bring them food.

Winter In The Forests

Wintertime is a very productive time in the forestry environment for the nature watcher, and a good time to come across a Fox looking for a meal, Crossbill feeding in the canopy, or perhaps a visiting Shrike from warmer European countries – a trend we are seeing more of in recent years. More importantly, it is a productive place not only for the specialists that are finding a living, but for the more common species relying on the forests to carry them through the colder months. Siskins, Crossbills and Redpoll all eak out a living when generally elsewhere food is scarce: their numbers bolstered with visitors migrating from the north of the country to lowland Britain. Birds normally associated with farmland and deciduous woodland such as Blue and Great tits, Chaffinch and Goldfinch gang up with their coniferous cousins and feed on the cones of the mature trees that are available when generally, other food sources may be in short supply. With the widely accepted view that the surrounding countryside is becoming less attractive for our native fauna through agricultural practices, in wintertime, the forests are becoming more attractive.

It is however this availability of cones (which equals seeds of course) that can come into question. This is born out by the fact that on occasions, they are not always there. As we will see in future chapters, the cyclic nature of cone production means that some years there are seeds to be eaten, and other years there are not. On top of this, some trees in a particular wood such as Larch for example may show fruit, and Spruce next door may be in a period where they do not bear any. From this, it is easy to see that the mixed species of tree types in woodland can generally hold populations of birds for longer periods over the year rather than singular tracts of mono-cultures. There is no difference with a pure Beech wood if compared to one with a mix of Beech, Oak, Sycamore and others in a deciduous woodland. Generally, in lowland Britain, this patchwork effect of differing cone producing trees has come about, over time perhaps through economics or on occasion deliberately manufactured probably without the needs of feeding birds even being considered. This mix can only be good for bird life, but also one species of tree can help another. It has been realized that mixes of conifers are useful in that Larch for example, may unlock nitrogen in the soil make-up for Spruce in some nutrient-poor areas.

These situations are important as it could mean that by observing the behavior of birds such as Finches, Tits or Crossbills, and leaving selected rows of older Larch or Spruce, birds could benefit on a local level, providing food when there is little or none for some distance. Action such as this can only increase the diversity of possible feeding opportunities for birds, and make the woodlands a more productive place for them, and for people who enjoy their presence.

Like our resident birds, our mammals such as Roe Deer find that the forests provide food and seclusion in the winter months.

Crossbill

If there is one bird that has captured the imagination with naturalists as a coniferous icon, then perhaps the Crossbill is it. For some it is an enigma. For many, study can be exasperating, both in terms of tracking them down and also in understanding their behavior. For taxonomists, those who figure out which species belongs to which family or group, there is constant debate as to which bird has developed from which species, and which is bona-fide in its own right, or just a sub-species. In any event, they are a joy to watch.

Their appearance is striking. The males are mainly red or orange with black wing coverts. The females, like a lot of coniferous birds are mainly green. Confusion can creep in though, because some males can be red with green! First impressions count as they say, and on first spotting them, a lot of people regard them as parrot-like. This can be mirrored in their feeding behavior, as often they can be seen taking a cone in their feet and eating from it like their exotic avian cousins, as in eating a monkey nut, for example.

Of course, as its name implies, it has a Crossed bill. The overlapping mandibles are adept at opening the overlapping cone scales which cover a conifer seed, which leave the tongue to winkle out the seed itself. When the bird has had enough, the cone is dropped, and it moves on to the next. Sometimes, it is possible to hear this, and it may be the only clue there is that a group is actually nearby. They can be very quiet. Unusual perhaps, because more often than not, there are a large group present. Seed wings that have been cast by feeding birds are another indication of their presence, as they creep around mouse-like in the canopy feeding. These can be seen spiraling to ground dispensed by the birds high in the canopy.

Most initial encounters with Crossbill though, are through their vocal attributes. Although they can be quiet and secretive as when feeding, generally they are noticeable when they move from one area to another. The "chip-chip" of Crossbills calling is the usual giveaway to their presence, most likely a flock of birds traveling high overhead.

Crossbills have been in Britain for centuries in one form or another. In Scotland, for example, there is Britain's' only endemic bird, the Scottish Crossbill, which is mainly found in the old Caledonian pine forests that are found around Speyside, and other similar habitats. These native pines are remnants left before major tree clearances took place over the last few thousand years or so. Another Crossbill variety exists here also, but in smaller numbers, the Parrot Crossbill. This is distinguishable from the Scottish because of its larger bill size, which aids its feeding on large pine cones. The Parrot can also be found in the Pines of Norfolk. It is here, that the taxonomists roughly agree. The bill size mainly separate the species, with the Scottish having slightly smaller a bill than the Parrot.

Common Crossbill

With the creation of the New Forests over the last century or so, a third species has emerged as probably the greatest in number. As its name implies, The Common Crossbill can be found across the British Isles as here it finds the introduced Spruce and other new tree colonists to its liking. This type of Crossbill has a slightly smaller bill than the Scottish, and thus finds access to its seeds easier.

Common though it may be in its name, it is in fact not such a common bird to see.

Initially it could be found in the south and east of the country, where the Victorians and the following generations of bird hunters and egg collectors would scour the lands for their trophies to line glass cabinet and wool-lined draw, but as new conifer plantations have matured around the country they have spread, although their numbers are never stable.

The green colouration of the hen Common Crossbill, which is sometimes mirrored by other small birds of the conifer forests, is in contrast to the brick-red of the male. Drinking is a regular part of their daily regime.

Common Crossbill's are great wanderers, and are thought to visit and colonize our shores from Scandinavia and Northern Europe, irrupting across the North Sea when food has failed to materialize in their native land. These visits are well documented, with birds staying on where there was food. On occasions, they then bred, but most returned to their native lands.

It is the very nature of coniferous seed production that has made the Common Crossbill a nomadic animal. Spruce seed is not produced on a regular basis, so when in some areas seed does not materialize, then they travel to areas that do, and this can be hundreds of miles. Some localities may not hold Crossbills for years, and then when conditions are right for seed production, they take advantage and stay while food is available.

When conifer trees are examined in detail, it becomes apparent why Crossbills lead such nomadic lives, as cone production can be complex. Having good seasons as well as bad, each species retains its seeds after production for varying times before they are released, although the birds can sometimes access them before they ripen.

Spruce for example, hold onto their seeds for nine months until the following spring before they are shed. Larch in contrast; until the first autumn - only three months. In mixed Spruce and Pine forests, Crossbills can breed when food is available almost all year round. In Northern Europe, they can breed in Spruce from August to May, and in pine from May to July.

In some areas where a blanket forest of single species has been implemented, it could be some time before the Crossbill can take advantage, as the food just may not be there. This may be because of a bad year as far as overall seed production is concerned, or that the trees are not mature enough. However, after trees have been harvested and a patchwork of different species have been added, over the course of time, then the chances of Crossbills using those particular forests are greatly increased. For example, if Spruce is in a stage of non seed production, then other trees nearby such as Larch may be, and support the birds. The flocking element is very strong in Crossbills, probably born through the need to stick together when it is necessary to find food some distance away, so contact with each other is important, hence their vocal nature.

Regarding breeding, with food supply being erratic, the Common Crossbill must therefore capitalize time when food is plentiful and nest when the time is right. From here we see that the bird has been recorded as breeding in most months of the year, and even will nest in winter time with several feet of snow.

The desire for the Crossbill to be part of a group or flock is strong, and a recurrent theme throughout its life, however the need to pair up to breed becomes ever stronger. Even on doing so, the other members of its species are never very far away, and often Common Crossbills nest in the same vicinity. Not in a colony, but close enough to interact from time to time. This can provoke serious in-fighting and tension as rival males and females for different reasons display, argue, and in contrast, even help each other in bringing up each others siblings.

It is here that the watcher can spend many hours with a stiff neck, looking at different pairs at the tops of high Spruce or Fir. Observations may provide insight as males attack others, bumping birds off the topmost fronds in battle for dominance, for example, but it can also leave one perplexed and confused as males return with food for their mates with other Crossbill in attendance. A picture of its life over time becomes apparent, but with the Crossbill there is always behaviour that proves unusual and at times baffling. Very often birds will use a "tooping" call which can be used when predators are near for example, but which can also be used in display or when Males are trying to show dominance within a group, or attracting a female. The Males themselves also have a musical song, used to advertise his presence to responsive female suitors and other males. When the pairs eventually decide to nest, the female initially starts the building process,

with the male in attendance. She selects small twigs from the forest floor and carries them to a chosen tree, usually at height, between 40 and 70 feet, out to a frond of spruce or similar conifer. He later joins in. This may not come to fruition, as she may change her mind, and try elsewhere.

Eventually the structure is finished with its cup like appearance, lined with wool, hair or grass and other soft materials, ready for the four or five eggs to be laid, one each day until the clutch is complete. The female initiates the brooding process and may start to cover the eggs from the second or third egg. As ever, the Common Crossbill can upset the trend, as some observers have found that they can incubate from when the first egg is laid. From this, generally the young hatch asynchronously, with a few days in age from the youngest to the oldest. Whether this is a strategy adopted for survival, such as in Owls, for example, but as a Finch, this is speculative. There is still much to learn.

When incubating, the male feeds the female for most part, and can fly some distance in search of food, even if there is apparent plentiful supply near at hand. Perhaps this nearby source is kept for later forays when the young are becoming mobile from the nest?

Juvenile common crossbill, like a lot of newly-fledged birds of the conifers, are dull and streked with sombre colours.

The young are in the nest for three weeks, being fed by both parents toward the end of their stay on a diet of mainly seed, as is to be expected. On this note, indeed, the main diet of the Crossbill is seed, gleaned from cones, but other items have been seen to be taken. Sometimes buds from newly emergent trees, and flower structures from deciduous trees such as Oak for example. They have also been seen on the ground beneath Beech, perhaps taking mast, or it may be that they were taking in grit, which a lot of seed-eaters pick up as a digestive aid. It has been observed that the female may eat some insect material prior to laying, and there is some speculation as to whether there is an element of insect food given to the young.

One of the best ways of seeing Crossbills are when they come to water. Most seed-eating birds drink frequently, and these are no exception. In areas where water is scarce, particularly when a long spell of dry, hot weather has evaporated most of the smaller pools that lie around the forest, then ponds and streams are utilized. They make a spectacular sight as they arrive en-mass, a whirl of reds, orange and greens, lining up to drink before flying back up to the canopy to feed once again. The more observant watchers may find that particular pools are favoured, surprisingly some of them being quite small.

With ingenuity, a hiding place can be fashioned out of natural materials found nearby, or use of one of the many hides that can be bought commercially, and close views can be obtained. Well worth the trouble, as they can then be fully appreciated.

Crossbill young take more time to become fledglings than other Finches, some 20 -25 days. When they are ready to leave, they are well feathered and can half-fly and creep around the foliage where their parents continue to feed them. They will still use the nest itself during the night as a dormitory, or can be brooded in times of bad weather. Later on, when they become more mobile, the brood is split between the male and female and each share the task of feeding. It may be here that they become mixed with other members of the overall flock that join them. Generally light brown or fawn, with streaks of darker brown over their plumage, it will be some time before they take on the full colours of adulthood. The bill at this time is straight too, as this is how they are when hatching, with the mandibles crossing over each other much later on, becoming true 'Crossbills'.

When seed supplies are very good, Crossbills may start to nest again soon after the young become more independent. At this time, the groups may comprise of a mixture of different birds at various stages. For example, as well as clearly defined pairs that are intent on nest building and mating, there may be parties of non-breeding males and females who are never too far away. Perhaps these birds had been unsuccessful in their attempts to breed, or may be birds that have bred some months before, and have had their broods. After all, it would be impossible to breed continuously as a pair.   Occasionally these may be seen assisting in the feeding of other birds' young. It has also been recorded that early fledglings may even assist in feeding the next generation that have come to fruition a few months after they have hatched.

This juvenile has started to take on the colouration of an adult.

The flocking behavior of Crossbills is always strong, and the tensions and hierarchies that exist are forever a factor that seems to predominate when these birds are breeding. With other Finches, it appears clear cut, as birds team up and nest, without interference from its kind. All pretty straight forward and usual. Not so with the Common Crossbill, where the flock ensures its survival. Because of the very nature of its erratic food supply, it needs the other members of the flock to find food as a collective to maximize its chances of survival.

For many years the enigma of Crossbill movements has been a subject of debate. It is generally thought that resident Crossbill in Britain have a short movement in summer, when most seeds are developing, and an area may lack food supply. They may only have to travel a relatively short distance before they possibly find food again. In contrast, they may also irrupt.

Here large numbers of Crossbills on the continent move large distances to other suitable areas. Some think this is in response again to food shortages such as a collapse in cone availability. Others put forward the idea that regions become overpopulated, so those birds look elsewhere for feeding and breeding opportunities. It may be a mixture of both. These irruptions are well documented from the 13th century by monks in St Albans, for instance, and many years since. They may settle and breed, perhaps bolstering our own populations, but generally, they return to their former areas. These initial dispersal's can take them in various directions from their original 'homelands' with no guarantee of even finding suitable places in which to find food.

Red Deer

To most, the Red Deer is an animal of the open moorlands. This is because it has adapted to the extensive deforestation that our country has endured over the centuries past. Perhaps surprisingly, it can and does live within our forests in surprisingly high numbers. For years, the population of Red deer was grossly underestimated, and is now seen in various areas as a significant pest. The thousands of miles of high fencing in Scotland are witness to this effect. The deer of the hill is a valuable amenity in supplying meat for consumption and as a shooting trophy for the estates of Scotland, where in part, a semi-managed situation occurs. As an animal of open ground, their numbers and general welfare can be monitored more easily than those of the forest.

Like all other deer, The Red is a browser. It can eat most herbage, including conifers, whether they are new saplings just planted on virgin ground, restocked, or well established forest up to head height. Pest or not, it is the largest of the British land animals, and is a well established member of our fauna. However these eating habits are also thought to be detrimental to other herbage, that other animals are dependent on within the forests. Initial studies show that inhibiting deer generally from some areas (and not just conifers) are beneficial to insects, particularly if they rely on specific plants that may be in short supply. Insects such as Butterflies are a case in point.

Most people are familiar with how the animal is involved in the autumn rut. While trying to keep a harem of females together, the males are engaged in a high octane mix of dominating inter-fighting, with head-on charging sometimes resulting in extremes of one of the contestants dying. It makes dramatic television footage that can keep us all on the edge of our seats; all this effort in the hope of breeding.

Visible on the open hill, but also carrying on within the seclusion of the forest, the rut is similar to that of the Fallow Deer. Likewise a herding animal, the social interaction is the same, and evolution has dictated that this strategy is an efficient method for the deer to get together. Usually, the two sexes spend most of their time apart, with the males forming bachelor parties away from the females with their offspring.

The loud calls or roars that resound from the Stags come about after the males split up and try to attract the females after returning to their areas. Stags are sexually mature after five years, and late August and early September is the time to find them starting the rut. Woodland populations of female Red deer are sexually mature after only a year, and give birth to a single calf eight months later in mid May to mid July.

Although the Red Deer is more prevalent in the uplands of Scotland, it can also be found in the South West, in Dartmoor and Exmoor, East Anglia, Cumbria and the New Forest, where of course it is a forest animal.

The population here in the south, kept to around a hundred individuals on FC land. Noticeable increases of this animal include the midlands, and South Wales, where forestry seems to be the catalyst for its spread.

The Future Of Forestry

We have seen that the Forestry machine has changed and adapted to various opinions and thoughts of the time. Probably this is to be expected, as any state owned industry is influenced by politics (which of course is influenced by public attitude) as well as economics. However, where initially it was just seen as a means of supplying timber, it is now also a valuable amenity for public leisure use, and with an increased interest as a wildlife resource. Public influences were initially slow, regarding this aspect, but in the last forty years or so this has significantly changed. With the establishment of codes of practice initiated by government and conservation bodies here and internationally, backed up by laws and planned with the intention to benefit wildlife, this aspect of conservation has come to the forefront. Examples of such can be seen up and down the country in the form of regional initiatives by the various forestry districts in partnership with their local wildlife bodies and councils.

Legislation involving our forest industry has become complex over the last fifty years or so, since the introduction of the Site of Scientific Interest scheme (SSSI's)in the late 1940's, to various countryside acts since, via the Nature Conservancy Council (now regionalized into Welsh, Scottish and English bodies).

International involvement came also, with the UNESCO (United Nations Educational, Scientific and Cultural Organisation) creating schemes such as The man and the biosphere programme in 1970. Wildlife laws and agreements also came to the fore when bodies

Nest boxes are not a new idea, and can be put to great effect within conifers for birds such as the Pied Flycatcher. Here, natural holes are in short supply, but they will take advantage if boxes are provided.

such as CITES gained influence. All this is great news for wildlife of course, as it has a direct impact on how our forests (and other habitats) are managed. With the climate of mistrust between forestry and conservation that was prevalent in the 70's and 80's, now we are seeing foresters becoming conservationists with changing attitudes and thinking coming from legislation. However, there are some in conservation that are still sceptical regarding wildlife interest within forestry.

There have always been initiatives to improve the lot for Wildlife. Some forestry has physically been turned back to its former existence, in this case - heathland in South Wales. Ponies are used to graze invasive herbage, negating the need for chemival control.

However, these attitudes reflecting foresters and conservationist's intent on improving the lot for wildlife did not happen overnight, and in some cases is nothing new. Even during those heated times of argument regarding the flow country and uplands in general with afforestation in the 1980's, there were initiatives going on.

For example, the improvement of habitat for birds such as Woodlark, Nightjar and other birds of the Brecklands of East Anglia using weed-killers to suppress grasses, were ideas that were acted upon years previously. With the introduction of myxamatosis and the subsequent decimation of the Rabbit population in that area, bare ground gradually reverted to sheep loving grassland, resulting in deterioration in heathland habitat.
Following on in the spirit of these early schemes to improve the lot for wildlife within the commercial forests, there are of course other ideas that can influence how we shape the habitat and attract wildlife which are far simpler than these, but can have just as many benefits and be implemented at a local level.

The provision of nest boxes is not a new idea, but can have implications that can affect birds and their populations. For example, most conifer woods lack old wood. Healthy trees are a natural aim of the forester, so rotten wood, which provides holes for species such as Pied Flycatchers are in short supply. In the past, the provision of boxes in suitable areas,(which also contain a low proportion of Broadleaf) have given these birds a toe-hold where they can live and breed. After time however, sadly these schemes had fallen by the wayside, and the birds disappeared probably because the people who started them have stopped for one reason or another. One successful scheme which is still in operation with Pied Flycatcher, however, is still running at the Nagshead Reserve in the Forest of Dean, being a joint operation between the Forestry Commission and the RSPB. Similar schemes are currently running with Ospreys in various parts of Britain, where nesting platforms have been erected, and Goldeneye nest boxes on Lochs within the forests. Paradoxically, these can be predated by another forest resident, the Pine Marten!
It had long been recognised that in the early stages of the New Forests' creation, in some areas the forests themselves were aesthetically unattractive. The planting up of land within the Lake district in the 1920's being one example. This aspect being of interest mainly to the countryside lovers who regarded the hard edges of the forests incongruous to the natural curves that the landscape generally offered - their input then starting the reshaping of the forests that were already there, and affecting those that may be created in the future. Other requirements, namely those needed by birds and other animals have over time come to the fore. The inclusion of a Broadleaf element can not only soften the geometric pattern that we all associate with some commercial forestry, but adds another attractive dimension to wildlife in general. These initiatives as we have seen, are nothing new, and have been going on for some time. We can only assume that similar actions will continue in the future.

Siskin

Probably the most noticeable of birds to spread as the New Forests started to develop around our shores, was the Siskin. Only found initially within the Scots pine in the north of the country, it is as good of an example as any, of how birds may take advantage of a 'new habitat'. A rich bottle green and yellow, the male's colour reflects the general background in which it is found; this being an adaptive feature that other birds also employ here, mainly as a means of blending in and becoming less noticeable to predators. The cock itself has a measure of black colouration around its head, varying to a degree, as some have a black bib, whereas other do not. The hen is much drabber, as is usually the case with females, being a buff brown or grey. With the Siskin preferring mainly to feed and nest in mature forestry, the population of the bird has not suffered the same fluctuation in numbers as its cousin the Redpoll. As we saw previous, numbers of this bird have mysteriously faded, but the Siskin has become a common bird found in most New Forests and the surrounding countryside.

A high single plaintive "sew" is its call as it flies, often in pairs or in groups of adults and young. The young themselves similarly to other fledgling coniferous song birds, are streaked and generally dull in colour.

Early spring is the time when the birds become particularly noticeable as the males sing and display high in the canopy. A butterfly-like flight from the tops can catch your eye. A musical twittering song sometimes finishing in a "wheezy" drawn out note distinguishes it from other songsters.

It isn't too long before pairs start to nest, the cup-like structure of twigs, wool, mosses and lichens is built high up on an outside branch. Four or five eggs, light blue/white, with brown and purple streaks, sometimes with blotches are laid. This initial breeding effort is often followed by another clutch a little later on.

A small finch, the Siskin is adept at feeding on seeds and from February to June it takes Pine, Spruce and Birch, but they also feed on plants such as Thistle, Meadowsweet or Mugwort in the summertime. In wintertime they can also be found in flocks with other birds such as Redpoll and Goldfinch, feeding on Alder along streams and rivers or in the mature conifer stands of Larch, particularly in lowland Britain.

Generally, the Siskin is sedentary in its movements, and will stay within the area where it has bred or in the same rough location in terms of any distance, as long as a food source can be found. Birch, Alder or conifer cone will keep them within a particular woodland, but tree seed production can be fickle, and they can move to another area if need be. With their general spread over the British Isles over the last fifty years or so, they have taken to feeding on garden bird tables, where nut dispensers have become popular.

As with the Redpoll, there can be a rough North to South movement of Scottish birds in autumn with birds here in search for better feeding opportunities. The general British population is bolstered in the winter months with birds migrating from Fenno-Scandia. These may not stay to breed, and after spending time on the Eastern side of our shores, may fly on to southern Europe and Iberia.

*Female
Siskin*

RESTRUCTURING

It is of no surprise, that we can and will improve the lot for birds and other animals not just in the New Forests of a commercial background, but of course for any other habitats be they gardens or wetlands. Present day interest from the public at large has made 'conservation' a topic that is important and it is generally felt that it is a good thing to do. With this in mind, more effort is being put in at national as well as local level within our commercial forests. Woodland restructuring is one big initiative, and as seen with the Lake District, has been around for a number of years. This theme has come to the forefront of recent policy regarding the commercial forests, particularly those owned by the state. Over the last few years the regional (country) forest bodies have laid out their vision on how the forests should be developed. Re-structuring plays a big part with reviving and conserving any existing ancient woodland. Broadleaf planting will play a big part in any new forests that are created and where possible, any coniferous plantation-style woodland would be 'improved'.

Could the introduction of continuous cover forestry
spell the end of an already succesful system?

A continuous woodland management structure would be implemented such as the Shelterwood system, where mature woodland would be harvested after being under-planted (or with natural regeneration) with similar trees, or, if an adjunct of conifer was to be used under Beech, for example, shade bearing conifers such as Western Hemlock or Red Cedar could be used. Thus, a continuous canopy would be maintained. Looked at as being more environmentally acceptable, mainly from an aesthetic point of view, it does have for a while a diverse layer of tree growth, but no bare ground or open stage for open loving birds and animals to use.

Group selection, is another method that is thought to be at the forefront of new restructuring within our forests of the future. Here small areas or pockets of mature wood are cut away within the forest, allowing enough light to enter and support the necessary light demanding trees such as Oak and Ash to be planted. This system is again looked on as being more environmentally acceptable, with possibly a greater diversity of tree species with a varied structure, but again with little open ground.

Some comments recently to surface regarding the clearfell method is being described as to be "difficult to deliver the full potential of environmental and social outcomes from healthy woodland systems."(Strategy for Welsh Woodlands). However, there are some important factors that come into play.

Ocassionally there is no great need for big machinery for harvesting, particularly when a sensative approach is better regarding any useful plantlife that is present, and need not be disturbed. as here in Pembrey, South Wales.

When we initially look at these other models, we can see perhaps it has advantages, mainly from aesthetic, leisure, or a viewpoint aspect. In reality though, systems such as the ones mentioned lack the difference of tree structure that birds in particular need (if we want a diverse mix). On another angle, could these other growing regimes deliver enough wood to be economically viable? Clear cut systems may not look the best in some peoples' eyes, but they are efficient and cost effective and they deliver huge volumes of timber. Conifer timber also has its advantages over broadleaf because it is more suited to the requirements of the building, pulp and board manufacturing industries.

However, studies and trials have looked into the viability of such systems along with cost implications and whether they could be adopted in our plantations as they are restructured over the coming years and some argue it is a policy worth pursuing. These methods may though suit some sites depending on certain criteria where the forest manager deems it may be successful.

Any form of bringing diversity to our woodlands, by introducing a greater range of tree species by re-structuring, should be welcomed, but in reality the present methods will be implemented for a long time to come, perhaps as in some locations, with a mixture of the two ideas being prevalent. Particularly in upland forests, where broadleaf introduction in some parts is unviable and, where vast areas are privately owned, some landowners just may not see it as a priority.

Grant aid is available however, to persuade investors whether they are farmers or companies, seeking to help clients when woodland is created. It is also hoped that this aid will offset any new developments regarding the new visions that are hoped to be achieved for our forests. Whether there will be enough money in the pot to reach these objectives, in recent times of austerity remains to be seen however.

There has always been a significant broadleaf influence within our commercial conifer forests in southern lowland areas, because after all, some of them were originally mixed Oak or Ash or Beech before they were cut and re-planted. If we walk around the commercial conifer plantations here, we will see the evidence of this. Perhaps in years to come we will see a gradual phasing out of the coniferous influence in the lowlands, with Broadleaf bringing in enough revenue to replace the conifers? However, if we eradicate the coniferous influences that have been created, we may risk losing the diversity that they bring.

There may be a stay of execution as regarding the loss of any open aspects being created in some areas. Normally, the tree stocks that are found within commercial forests are of a healthy disposition. This though does not take into account for the fact that sometimes large scale disease can break out. This is happening at the moment with the establishment of the Phytophthora fungus which seems to be rapidly establishing itself. Initially found in the south west, it now threatens the Forest of Dean, where thousands of trees are being felled in the hope of halting the spread. Wales has some elements of infection too.

Although rare, these situations create large clear spaces, in which at least our open-loving birds can exploit. Arguably too, they open up views for the general nature lover that otherwise would not be available.

RED SQUIRREL

Although the bulk of the population reside within Scotland, the Red Squirrel can be found at other locations within Britain. Mainly an animal of mature forestry, it can also be seen within commercial forests besides the Old Caledonian Pine forests of the North. Found across Britain in times gone by, it has become marginalised to small areas chiefly dominated by former FC land. These areas are now mainly coniferous, but it used to be also found within Broadleaf woodlands in the past, where it could feed on nuts such as Hazel, Beech, Oak as well as their flowers.

Red or a russet brown of course best describes the colouration of this small mammal, but there are exceptions, from ginger to others being much darker, even to a black. In the summer months for example, some individuals' tales take on an almost blonde appearance. Their ear-tufts can disappear in this season too, as the animal has a much thinner coat. At around 20cm in length, with an extra 18cm of tail, it can look smaller, as it characteristically sits nibbling on a food item; its tail curving over its back.

Precocious, they can have litters at any time of the year, with September and November being quieter months.

The summer coat of the Red Squirrel is thinner than its winter one, with a much lighter coloured tail, and and very little in the way of ear-tufts.

They do not stay together as a pair, as males mate with several females in his area, with the female alone being responsible for bringing up the two to three kittens, born after a pregnancy of 45 to 48 days. Noisy and noticeable in its courtship, sites such as Formby in Lancashire, or Brownsea Island in Dorset can be good places to see such activity.

Here agile chasing between the sexes can be seen, travelling across canopy or up, down and around the trees boughs. Peak mating is around January, with the majority of litters born in the March.

A football-sized collection of twigs make up
the outside dimensions of the drey

Red Squirrels build dreys, which are shelters of twigs and bark in which to nest and sleep. The ball-shaped structure can be built from scratch, or on the foundations of an old birds nest such as Crow, or Magpie, and can last for a few years with refurbishment. They can also be found to reside in dens. Old Woodpecker, or rotten holes within trees can be used, but within the new commercial environment, a drey would generally be the norm, as rotten wood is in short supply.

There is an element of drey sharing between Red Squirrels, where in cold weather several individuals may occupy a single space, supposedly in an effort to keep warm. The squirrel does not hibernate ; an aspect that some people have found suprising, and can be seen at

all times of the year. Masters of their arboreal, or tree loving environment, they are able to perform spectacular jumps of up to six metres within the canopy as they travel.
The longer hind legs coupled with shorter front, give the perfect make-up for this tree-top existence, the latter acting as shock absorbers as they land.

One question that people always seem to ask about the squirrel is: Why has the Red Squirrel become so uncommon? The main aspect has been mainly blamed on the introduction of the Grey Squirrel in the 19th century, but it is not the whole story. It is generally thought that the introduced species is more aggressive than the former Red, and has just pushed it out. A look at old distribution maps of the two, certainly gives weight to this, with the Grey inhabiting areas where the Red has disappeared, but when examining both their lifestyles, we can see the Grey is far more successful when it comes to feeding. For example, the Red prefers mature seed to feed on, but we can find that the Grey will also take the un-ripened seed, so its feeding opportunities are extended.

Some years ago, it was realised that the Red was also prone to suffer from a gut parasite which may have been instrumental in its decline in the 1920's. Following on from this, disease again, as the situation was exasperated by the paropox virus. Thought to be stress-related, the inclusion of a major competitor such as the Grey Squirrel would have not helped. As a result, any fall in areas where Red squirrel were to be found, would have probably been filled with the Grey. Severe winters are also thought to have taken a part.

Recently, a new threat has come to the fore which is far more disturbing for the Red Squirrel. A new virus has emerged and has decimated numbers in some parts. Carried and spread by the Grey, but does not effect it as badly. There being no known cure against this squirrel pox, perhaps at the moment, the regionalization of some populations may help, if the Grey Squirrel is prevented from being able to mix. With this in mind, culls of the Grey are being undertaken around the areas Reds are known to be found, in the hope of preventing any further spread of the disease. Coincidently, with the Grey Squirrel thought to be a major pest in the development of commercial forestry, it is listed to be controlled from this angle, particularly in areas such as lowland forestry where a greater mix of conifer and broadleaf occurs. Controls such as culling are a subject in which some people find distasteful, especially if the animals in question are attractive, such as the Grey Squirrel. However, looking into a broader context such as their influences on other species, perhaps we can see that in some cases it seems justified. Grey squirrels can have negative influences not only on growing stock such as trees as well as Red Squirrels, but also on birds such as the Crossbill, where they can predate eggs and nestlings.

With the Red Squirrel being only found within certain areas around Britain, studies have been carried out to find out what criteria favour them. Clocaenog, in north Wales is one place where such a programme has taken place. It is thought from this that the Red Squirrel does well in larger coniferous forests, with little or no Broadleaf influence, (which attracts the grey). Feeding on cone seeds, the squirrels' population was found to vary in number with the cyclical supply of seed that the trees produce, but would feed on a variety, such as Larch, or Norway Spruce when available - but Sitka was generally shunned.

The Greys preferred the broadleaf elements, and were transient within the conifers. It was also noted that the Reds were tolerant of forestry working, such as thinning, moving out to other suitable areas while the work was going on, then returning when the work was over.

Strategies could be formulated from this and other studies that could help in the meantime, but could the Red once more play a part within its former homelands in the future? Perhaps the shyer, less robust make up of the Red Squirrel compared to the successful Grey may mean that it could still be confined to the areas that it still inhabits today. Then again, the larger commercial conifer forests may prove a salvation.

CALEDONIA

Could the Future for some, perhaps be in commercial forestry?

It is five o'clock in the morning and almost fifty people take it in turns to glimpse a male Capercaillie displaying - A brief view that will stay in their minds forever. This rare bird, the largest grouse in the world, can be found in relics of Caledonian pine, mainly found in Scotland within our British Isles. Places such as Abernethy, in Speyside, where this particular organized spectacle is taking place. Scots Pine here is not harvested as a crop, and so has no commercial value as a raw material, but reflects monitory value nonetheless, via tourism.

This return then, comes from a different route to the growing and harvesting of timber which we have previously encountered, but has a direct benefit financially to the people who work within the forests there,whether they are teaching skills such as cycling, bird watching, trecking, or providing accommodation and hospitality nearby.

The value of this type of woodland is not only as an amenity for physical outdoor pursuits, but also in the species of wildlife that live within its boundaries. It contains birds and animals that in some cases are not usually found elsewhere, and represent strongholds for some that cannot be replaced. They have become dependent to a greater extent on this type of habitat. Or have they?

Caledonian, or Scotts pine is the only native pine within British shores. It has been here for thousands of years, and for the most part only can be found in larger tracts in Scotland with only some 16000 hectares remaining. The creatures that are special to the forests here have been a part of them for probably just as long, and in some cases the forests have actually shaped the creatures themselves that they can live within them.

The Caledonian forests though are finite in respect to their size and suitability for the specials that live within. Sometimes they are viewed as too small perhaps to sustain viable populations, so other habitats must be made available. Once the major tree inhabitant in the north, the pine forests have succumbed to constant harvesting over the last few thousand years, and now hang on in just these last few places.

Species which live within this coniferous enclave, have been recognised in needing attention and help, due to their relative fragility of numbers. One bird in particular being the Capercaillie.

Glen Affric.

Capercaillie

The Capercaillie was once a bird found within Scotland in good numbers, but became extinct in the mid 18th century. However, it was then reintroduced some one hundred years later, as like some other members of our native wildlife it found itself becoming extinct through shooting and habitat changes. Since then, its range has shrunk where it now inhabits mainly old Caledonian pine woods. Here an open forest is indicative of these native pines, which has a rich under-story of Bilberry and other dwarf shrubs along with mosses and pollen cones.

Interspersed, are boggy areas, supporting a rich environment of plants such as Cotton grass, sedges and rushes, which in turn house a variety of insect life. And of course there are the pines. Capercaillie, mainly eat the needles in winter and spring with a mixture of all these differing areas providing the necessary conditions for them to thrive.

Unfortunately, native pine woods such as this type form only a small proportion of woodland today, and since the bird was reintroduced, it has struggled for various reasons and is now hanging on with an uncertain future. However, the Capercaillie problem is solvable, and initiatives have been undertaken to address the problems that exist with an aim to bolster the existing population and increase its footing.

Part of the problem for Capercaillie, as we have seen, is that they require and use differing parts of the forest at different times of the year, and perhaps in the past the inclusion of blanket forestry has not helped. This recognition has highlighted the issue, and hopefully it also may be its salvation in the future.

Commercial Scots pine, which although set up initially as plantation in style, is being developed to favour Capercaillie, and as in the case with its cousin, the Black Grouse, action plans have been devised to try and solve their problems and increase the spread of the bird. These plantation woodlands are usually surrounding the old Caledonian enclaves, so it is hoped that they in future will expand their requirements.

Restructuring and opening up the woodlands, allowing more light can enter the floor, and stimulating the growth of Bilberry and other plants to thrive can replicate the older pine habitat.

Wet areas are also developed. Here, hens with chicks can find the insect life they need, which is crucial to get the young established. Where woods are being thinned out, and clearings and glades are formed, some stands of denser conifer are allowed, along with piles of brash, so that families can shelter in bad weather - a major problem for nesting birds and young in wetter spring months.

The problem of Deer, which are regarded as a pest to forestry, has in the past been partly dealt with by fencing. This has had a detrimental effect for Capercaillie, with many fatalities to the bird as they fly into them. Some have been taken down, and others made more visible by the addition of extra panelling along their lengths.

This extending of the Capercaillies range may eventually join with other relics of Caledonian pine remnants and afford larger areas for the birds to hopefully flourish. Creation of corridors has long been a strategy for increasing and joining habitat for various animals in other areas, so it is hoped that this idea will help here.

Other birds of the Old Caledonian pines also seem to benefit from the plantations that were for years to be thought of no great importance. The Scottish Crossbill, Britain's only endemic bird has taken to Lodgepole Pine, particularly in the North East Highlands. Birds can be good at adapting and using other environments if they have to change, and the maturing Pines here seem to offer conditions for the Crossbill in which to live. This area of Sutherland and Caithness was much scorned upon when originally planted as encroaching on moorland loving birds, but now houses different rarities.

Similarly, the Crested Tit can also find the commercial plantation to their liking. Scots Pine features significantly as a commercial crop around the Old Granny type and they can be frequently found amongst them. Again thought needs to be put in regarding this, and tweaking the general regime can bring these birds into living permanently within the commercial environment. Providing old rotting wood for example, a pre-requisite for Cresties to nest in, is essential if they were to stay permanently.

The opening up of woodland such as this in Inshriach, on Speyside, hopefully encourages plants to grow such as Blaeberry and provide food for Capercaillie.

Crested Tit

High Summer

Spring rolls in to summer within the forest, and from a wildlife watching perspective these (hopefully) balmier months can be a little quiet in the calendar. Gone are the days where the birds in particular have dropped their singing oratories, when it is relatively easy to see and find them. Most birds have left their nests after this initial rush of activity in the early half of the year, and other animals are also looking after their offspring, becoming elusive and secretive. It is perhaps at this time that the coniferous forests earn their miss-earned theme as barren and empty. However, a visit to any deciduous woodland can give a similar conception. It is at this time we need to change tack if we wish to see and observe. Rather than close in on any activity that we can hear or see, as we did in the earlier months, we need to sit and wait for any potential wildlife to come to us.

The woodlands are a good source of food for birds such as tits at this time of year as they provide much needed protein to build young bodies for the forthcoming harder winter months. Often traveling in parties, Coal tits will join Blue and Great, as well as others such as Willow Warbler and Chiffchaff as they travel along through the canopy. The trees at this time of course have developed their full leaf-covering capacities and along with any ground herbage, all offer excellent cover for small birds and mammals in which to hide. By sitting for a while and not becoming noticeable yourself, then you are maximizing your chances on observing any animals that are moving around. Birds such as the tits for example, tend to patrol areas they are familiar with and eventually, return to places they have found food in before.

Any watercourse can only help in this way, and time spent near any ponds or wet flushes particularly in times of water shortage should attract attention and a mix of birds, mammals and insects. Gaining a perspective of how close one can get of course comes with experience. Some birds and animals are more confiding than others; birds such as Sparrowhawks can see any movement if you are near and are off in a blink of an eye, but Crossbill on the other hand can be very confiding and a closer view may be rewarded. Building a hiding place can be a satisfying way for closer viewing of course. Stalking can also be used to some effect. It is at this time, for example that young Buzzards are particularly vocal and sit atop of trees and shout to be fed. Juvenile Sparrowhawks are also quite approachable as they shout from within the canopy and with these situations, we can often use the leaf cover to get a little closer as they are preoccupied with food.

Birds such as the Sparrowhawk can be seen in the drier months especially
at water-holes such as ponds. A hide is best used as the birds are easily put off.

The conifer forests that are in effect nature reserves are great places to watch wildlife.
One attractive feature to most of these areas is the lack of people who visit them, thus
increasing your chances in observing. Perhaps this may change in the coming years as the
'secret' gets out, but for the most part, one could walk around the network of roads and
paths within the forest and not see another person, save for the odd dog-walker.
Getting off the paths into rougher ground is the answer to being undisturbed by others,
this especially if you want to commit time and resource in setting up bird feeders or hides
for example.

Pine Marten

In general, we initially think of the Pine Marten, a creature that lives in the Caledonian Pine forests of Northern Scotland. This initial observation is true, but in reality it can be found across a wide area of Scotland itself, and possibly elsewhere within the British Isles.

Their story is a fascinating one, as various conservation bodies dispute its existence in England and Wales to begin with, and whether or not it should be reintroduced if it doesn't!

Slender in appearance, this Marten Cat, as it was known in past times, was widespread across Britain. Trapping for its fur, general persecution, along with game keeping practices, and loss of habitat has seen its numbers fall substantially around our shores and until about 1915, it was restricted to the wilder areas of Scotland. The Highlands being the center of the main population, action was taken in the 1980's to expand its range, and some animals were captured, and trans-located to the Galloway area by the Forestry Commission to establish another group. These have flourished within the New Forests which had been created there, in these last fifty years or so.

But what of the animal itself? It is a member of the Weasel or Mustilid family, and in general shape it has the appearance of a big Stoat or Pole Cat. It is bigger than the two in reality, and is about the size of a small domestic cat. An omnivore, it is able to live on a variety of plant and animal food items, apparently in some ways competing with the Fox. This catholic taste in food requirements should indicate an animal that should do well within our countryside if given a chance, but what of the reality?

Although the main population of Pine Marten is recognized to be found within Scotland, it has long been thought that other populations reside within England and Wales. The occasional sighting and scat find has fueled the debate that there are some Martens to be found 'south of the border', but dispite various attempts to verify this, the situation still remains unclear.

A co-ordinated scat collection at various hot spots around the country, with subsequent samples testing for DNA in the last few years has not come up with anything really concrete in establishing whether there are other meaningful populations. In view of this, The Vincent Trust, an independent wildlife organization, which promotes wildlife conservation, has come up with a strategy in the hope of reinvigorating the animal's fortunes outside of Scotland.

A comprehensive monitoring plan is the first response, in the hope of any remaining animals increasing in number and bolstering themselves. The other strategy, would be to introduce animals in a structured programme. There are fears attached to this idea though, as any reintroduction may be counter-productive to any genetic stock that might exist, but this thought has been generally dismissed, as any occurring animals may have been influenced by Scottish stock or by other animals from outside the British Isles. Any introduction would have to include IUCN guideline requirements however, which is a framework that closely monitors such work and validates what impact any such actions have on already established animals. However, as we have seen from the Galloway initiative, this could work.

Usually a solitary animal, the Pine Marten needs a lot of woodland in which to operate. Females have their own home ranges, and males will visit these and other territories that females occupy. The size of these ranges varies with habitat and food availability, with the males occupying territories roughly twice to three times the size of its intended suitors. Sizes can range from approximately 33sq/km for upland Spruce forest in Galloway, to 3 per sq/km in the case for lowland forestry in the Inverness area.

With males visiting various females during the breeding season, it comes perhaps of no surprise that they themselves do not take part in rearing the young. Mating around July-August, the females bring up the young on their own when they are born in the March or early April, the following year.

A mechanism of delayed implantation occurs, where five to six months is followed by a gestation period of about thirty days.

Being mainly nocturnal in habit, getting to grips in seeing Pine Martens may take time and effort on the watchers part, but in Scotland they can be seen in the daylight hours, especially in the summer months. With a sweet tooth, they can be attracted to baited areas similar to bird feeding stations, using jam or peanut butter. Chocolate-covered raisins are also a favourite.

The animals have two coats which vary in colour. In summer they are chocolate brown with a creamy-yellow chest patch, but in September, the animal starts to moult into its winter pelage, which is much lighter than the previous one. Now at a level that is perhaps at the brink of whether the animal can be detected outside of Scotland, and if in sufficient numbers to form sustainable populations, the New Forests could play a big part if the path of reintroduction was taken. Perhaps ironic, that the bigger forests that were initially criticized in swallowing up so much countryside, whether upland moorland or lowland heath, may be a salvation for the Pine Marten in the future if they were given the chance.

It is no surprise that any animal may impact with another through predation, as has been described in a food chain. This of course has a varying degree on each of the inhabitants of that chain, with the overall effect reaching a stable level which is generally seen as beneficial in the long-run even to those that are being preyed upon. This comes into question with some, regarding interaction with other rare and endangered species however. The Pine Marten has long been associated with this thought.

Being generally restricted within its range in Scotland, it can have an impact on other birds and animals that too are viewed as in need of help in increasing their number: the Goldeneye being a case in point. As mentioned previously, they can predate, and thus negate the workings of well intended conservationists and foresters by raiding nest-boxes set up for the birds.

The big question and dilemma here is, what can we do? This situation is hampered of course by the fact that we are dealing with two species found in generally low numbers, and it could be seen as ludicrous to try and control either species.

The Pine Marten is excellently adapted for living within the canopy.

Over the last few decades, speculative statements have been published by some people such as Gamekeepers, that Pine Martens have a negative effect on animals such as Capercaillie in that they are detrimental to their numbers, with the view that Pine Martens should be controlled. These statements can be disputed however, with movements such as the RSPB verifying through study, that this is not the case.

Of Great Value? : Postscript

We have seen how that the commercial forests of Britain, perhaps initially through ignorance as being painted as of no importance wildlife, can attract and sustain important populations of birds and animals. In some cases they may be common in general, but also encompass specialists that would otherwise not be around in any number if the New Forests had not created in the first place.

Viewed as places of leisure by some, sterile plantations by others, they can also be seen as important refuges for wildlife in times where space is becoming a premium for both people and animals outside of the forest, as biodiversity is lost due to pressures such as development and intensive farming. Initially set up to supply timber for us all, the New Forests deliver this primary aim, but also provide places in which animals can survive and prosper. Our state-owned forestry commission is coming up to the end of its first centenary, and with future political visions and changing policies, how will the wildlife inhabitants be influenced in the next one hundred years?

About The Author And Photography

DAVE LOCK has been photographing wildlife for over twenty five years.
The idea for this book came from working on a program on the theme for Welsh television in the 1990's – *Spirit of the Wildwood.*
Impressed by what the commercial forests can offer, he has been watching and photographing their inhabitants since. Finishing his 'proper job' some years ago, he now concentrates full time on photography, and watching animals.

"The photographs in the book have been taken over the last fifteen years or so, and span both film and digital media. Kodachrome and Fuji slide film were used before moving to digital capture in 2006. All are wild and free except the following: Pine Marten, Stoat (pg 21), Sparrowhawk (pg 82) and Long Eared Owl.
Some species featured are long term projects, such as Goshawk and Crossbill. The nature of these animals dictating that it can take time to secure pictures. For example, the nesting Goshawk, usually require tower hides with scaffolding, and special licences must be procured before photography can begin. The nomadic lifestyle and unreliability of Crossbill being another challenge the photographer has to consider. Some subject matter of course comes from observation and general background knowledge gleaned from experience over the years, but other pictures could only come from the involvement of various people who have kindly helped over times past".

Thanks to:

Colin Elliot	Steve Smith
Adrian Thomas	Derek Gowe
Jerry Lewis	Rory Richardson
Colin Leslie	Wayne Fitter
Dr. E P Toyne	Chris Sperring
Herman Ostrosnic	Tony Phelps

Further Reading / Bibliography

Aichele, D	Wild Flowers	1975
Avery, Leslie	Birds and Forestry	1990
Bouchard, Moutou	Observing British and European Mammals	1989
Brown, L	British Birds of Prey	1976
BTO	The New Atlas of Breeding Birds	
Condry, W	The Natural History of Wales	1981
Forestry Commission	Crossbills Leaflet 36	1963
	Forest Nature Conservation Guidelines	1990
	Wildlife Rangers Handbook	1994
Harris and Harris	Wildlife Conservation in Managed Forests and Woodlands	1987
Holm, J	Squirrels	1987
Hosking and Newbury	Birds of the Night	1945
Hosking and Read	Eggs and Fledglings in colour	1971
	Nesting Birds	1967
Kenward R	The Goshawk	2006
Lewis et al	The Birds of Gwent	2008
Mammal Soc, Birks	The Pine Marten	2002
Mathews	British Mammals	1952
NCC	Birds, Bogs and Forestry	c1980
Nethersol-Thompson D	Pine Crossbills	1975
Newton I	Finches	1972
	The Sparrowhawk	1986
Orchal J	Forest Merlins in Scotland	1992
Peterken G	Woodland Conservation and Management	1981
Pforr and Limbrunner	The Breeding Birds of Europe	1982
Simms	Woodland Birds	1990
Stephen D	Watching Wildlife	1963
Toyne E P	Studies on the Ecology of the Northern Goshawk	1994
Vincent Wildlife Trust	The Distribution and Status of the Polecat in the 1990's	1999

www... The Forestry Commission website is a great place to find information whether it is species specific or just what is happening in your area. www.forest.gov.uk.

INDEX :

Adder **13**
Acid Rain **60**
Available cut 10
Biodiversity Action Plnanning 50,134
Black Grouse 49
Brash 9
BTO 73
Buzzard 89,95,98
Butterflies 90/1

Caledonian 105,126,131
Capercaillie 89,133,137,143
Chaffinch 17,89
Chinese Water Deer 57
Coal Tit 86
Continious Cover 122
Crested Tit 135
Crossbill 66,102,104,129,135
Crow 50,78,84

Deer 26,46,135
Dipper 59,60
Divers 66
Drainage 60
Dreys 127

Fallow Deer 53
Farming 52
Fox 46,50,52
Flow Country 36,74

Goldcrest 70,72,87
Goldfinch 66,91,102
Goldeneye 59,66,142
Goshawk 94
Greater Spotted Woodpecker 16
Green Woodpecker 44
Grey Squirrel 128/9
Grey Wagtail 59

Heathland 9,31
High Seats 56

Legislation 115/6
Leisure Activities 93

Lek 50
Lesser Redpoll 34,120
Linnet 46,91
Mammal Numbers 73
Merlin 78, 85
Muntjac Deer 57
Myxamatosis 118

Nightjar 18,89,118
Nest Boxes 116

Pied Flycatcher 116,118
Pine Marten 139
Pond Creation 63,66
Private Companies 31,38

Red Deer 74,113
Red Grouse 75/6
Red Squirrel 125
Re-stocking 31,114
Roe Deer 26,27,113
RSPB 50
Rutting   29,55

S E Owl 33
Sika Deer 57
Siskin 34,66,91
Song Thrush 16
Sparrowhawk 42,80,95,137/8
Spotted Flycatcher 89
Stoat 13,21,74
Studies 72,76,84

Tawny Owl 13
Tree Pipit 11

Water Rail 61
Whitethroat 46,72
Whinchat 40
Wildlife and Countryside Act   38
Wildlife Rangers/Foresters 56,63,91
Willow Warbler 73,137
Windthrow 89,93
Wood uses 25

Printed in Great Britain
by Amazon